RADICAL POLITICAL ECONOMY

For too long radical political economy has suffered for lack of a coherent alternative to formal Marxian economic theory. People have had to choose between (1) continuing to use a formal model based on the labor theory of value as Marx developed in *Capital* to justify and retain one's opposition to capitalism, or (2) abandoning the formal Marxian framework as outdated, and risk losing a critical evaluation of capitalism. *Radical Political Economy: Sraffa Versus Marx* provides readers with a third choice.

A point-by-point comparison of Sraffian and Marxian treatments of prices, profits, technological change, economic crises, environmental sustainability, and the moral case against capitalism, are presented in six core chapters. They explain how the Sraffian treatment surpasses the formal Marxian treatment in every case. Both Marxian and Sraffian theories are presented in a highly accessible way, while large professional literatures are thoroughly referenced throughout.

Marx was not the first, but remains the greatest, critic of capitalism, and richly deserves his place in history. However it is time to use intellectual tools unavailable to Marx in the nineteenth century to improve upon his formal analysis. This book is of great importance to those who study Sraffa and Marx, as well as academics and students who are interested in political economy, the history of economic thought, and economic and philosophical theory.

Robin Hahnel is Professor Emeritus at the Department of Economics, American University Washington DC, USA. He is also the Co-Director of Economics for Equity and the Environment and has published widely in the fields of radical political economy and environmental economics.

RADICAL POLITICAL ECONOMY

Sraffa Versus Marx

Robin Hahnel

Routledge
Taylor & Francis Group

LONDON AND NEW YORK

First published 2017
by Routledge
2 Park Square, Milton Park, Abingdon, Oxon OX14 4RN

and by Routledge
711 Third Avenue, New York, NY 10017

Routledge is an imprint of the Taylor & Francis Group, an informa business

British Library Cataloguing in Publication Data
A catalogue record for this book is available from the British Library

Library of Congress Cataloging in Publication Data
Names: Hahnel, Robin, author.
Title: Radical political economy : Sraffa Versus Marx / Robin Hahnel.
Description: 1 Edition. | New York, NY : Routledge, 2017. | Includes
bibliographical references and index.
Identifiers: LCCN 2017001421| ISBN 9781138050020 (hardback) |
ISBN 9781138050037 (pbk.) | ISBN 9781315169149 (ebook)
Subjects: LCSH: Economics. | Technological innovations--Economic
aspects. | Capitalism--Moral and ethical aspects. | Marx, Karl,
1818-1883--Political and social views. | Sraffa, Piero--Political and
social views.
Classification: LCC HB171 .H2354 2017 | DDC 330.15/3--dc23
LC record available at https://lccn.loc.gov/2017001421

ISBN: 978-1-138-05002-0 (hbk)
ISBN: 978-1-138-05003-7 (pbk)
ISBN: 978-1-315-16914-9 (ebk)

Typeset in Bembo
by Taylor & Francis Books

CONTENTS

PREFACE

Marx deserves his place in history as the greatest critic of capitalism. Marx opened our eyes to how the economic sphere of social life exerts a powerful influence over the political, cultural, and reproductive spheres of social life. Marx gave intellectual support to workers' instinct that capitalism systematically exploits them. And Marx reminded us that life beyond capitalism, where workers manage and coordinate their economic activities themselves, democratically, fairly, and efficiently, is a real possibility.

However a great deal has happened since Marx died in 1883. There are 133 years of world history – some of which, such as the Soviet perversion of the socialist vision, and capitalism's recovery from the Great Depression, would have come as a great surprise to Marx. And there have been new intellectual discoveries as well, some of which, such as proof of the Frobenius–Perron theorem in mathematics, and modern, egalitarian, philosophical theories of distributive justice, provide us with intellectual tools unavailable to Marx.

It is time to acknowledge that Marx's early attempt to fashion a formal economic theory of price and income determination in capitalism based on a "labor theory of value," and elaborate a Hegelian "critique" of capitalism can now be surpassed. Not surpassed by neoclassical theory, which only disguises the origins of profits and their lack of moral legitimacy. Surpassed instead by a modern reworking of classical economics along the lines pioneered by Piero Sraffa (1960), centered on the production and distribution of the physical economic "surplus," and by a modern egalitarian philosophical theory of distributive justice.

This book argues that Sraffian theory can now provide a stronger basis for radical political economy in the twenty-first century than formal Marxian economic theory for a number of reasons:

- Sraffian theory is devoid of embarrassing inconsistencies which plague Marxian formal theory which apologists for capitalism exploit.
- Because it uses familiar economic and philosophical concepts – rather than a conceptual apparatus abandoned long ago by all except Marxists – Sraffian theory is more intelligible to economists, philosophers, and lay audiences today.
- Sraffian theory and the "Fundamental Sraffian Theorem" show more clearly why capitalists are parasites living off the work of others than does Marxian theory and the "Fundamental Marxist Theorem."
- Formal Marxian economic theory misleads us to search for non-existent crises which distracts us from focusing attention on actual sources of crisis in capitalism.
- Finally, no theory unsuited to analyzing the increasingly problematic relation between human economic activity and the natural environment will attract allegiance as the twenty-first century unfolds. Unlike the Marxian labor theory of value which is ill-suited to incorporating inputs from "nature" into our formal analysis, the Sraffian framework easily accommodates natural resources and rents into an explanation of price and income distribution. Moreover, recent developments demonstrate how Sraffian theory can facilitate a rigorous analysis of what ecological economists call environmental throughput, allow us to formulate sufficient conditions for achieving environmental sustainability in a multi-good economy, and sort out the "sense" from the "nonsense" in the steady-state and de-growth literatures.

This book examines six topics: In each topic area both the Marxian and Sraffian treatments are presented and compared. Those six core chapters are preceded by an introduction that pays full homage to Marx, but argues that it is time to improve on his formal modeling, and followed by a conclusion summarizing the advantages of a radical version of modern Sraffian theory.

Since this book is intended for a broad audience, I will use a simple, two sector version of both the Marxian and Sraffian models which requires nothing more than simple algebra, and I will emphasize intuitive explanations for all important results, referring readers to endnotes for more complicated calculations and suitable sources for proofs of key theorems.

INTRODUCTION

For too long radical political economy has suffered for lack of a coherent alternative to formal Marxian economic theory. For too long those dis-enamored with the economics of competition and greed have had only two choices: (1) Continue to use a formal model based on the labor theory of value as Marx developed it in *Capital* – to justify one's opposition to capitalism. Or (2) abandon the Marxian framework as outmoded – and risk losing a rationale for rejecting capitalism as fundamentally flawed. This book is dedi-cated to providing the next generation fighting against the destructive effects of financialized, neoliberal, global capitalism a third choice: (3) A modern, rigorous, logically sound, and profoundly radical version of Sraffian economics.

Sraffian theory uses concepts and tools familiar and acceptable to economists and philosophers in the twenty-first century. A radical version of Sraffian theory can be every bit as critical of capitalist inequality as Marxism. Sraffian theory suggests no mythical theories of crisis, allowing us to focus on real sources of instability and crisis in capitalist economies. And finally, unlike Marxian theory, the Sraffian framework proves to be well suited to addressing what is arguably already the paramount issue of the twenty-first century – environmental sustainability. However, before beginning it is appropriate to pay homage to Marx, who in all likelihood will forever remain the greatest critic of capitalism.

Prior to Marx nobody understood how much the way we organize our interrelated economic activities affects the way we think and behave. In the hands of some of his disciples lumping the political, cultural, and reproductive spheres of social life into a single "superstructure," and insisting that the "economic base" always exerts more influence over the superstructure than vice versa, may have become an obstacle to a fuller understanding of how human societies function.[1] But to blame the prophet for the sectarian excesses of his disciples is unfair.

Nobody has provided more support to workers' sense that capitalists rob them of part of what they produce and suppress their abilities to manage and coordinate their own laboring capacities. Even if it proves that we now have better tools and ways to explain how and why the capitalist employment relationship is exploitative than were available to Marx 150 years ago, this does not diminish the magnitude of what he accomplished in this regard: Nobody has provided stronger ideological support for the labor movement and its cause than Marx.

And finally, Marx more than anyone else emphasized that capitalism was merely the latest in a series of flawed, class-divided economic systems that have come and gone throughout history. And like other human creations before it, there is no reason people cannot replace it with a better economic system, a classless economy in which workers and consumers coordinate a rich and productive division of labor among themselves – democratically, fairly, and efficiently.

For all this, and more, we owe Marx an unpayable intellectual debt, and nothing in this book should be interpreted as implying otherwise.

In chapter 1 the Marxian and Sraffian theories of prices are presented and compared. Sraffian theory derives relative prices in capitalism directly from the technologies used to produce different goods and services and whatever hourly wage rate workers are able to win. Marxian theory assumes a subsistence wage rate, derives labor values from technologies, and then transforms labor values into "prices of production." The chapter argues that not only are labor values unnecessary, i.e. redundant, they also mislead analysts about the process of price formation in capitalism.

In chapter 2 the Marxian and Sraffian theories of profit are presented and compared. Explaining the origin of profits is an important issue in radical political economy. And the fact that neoclassical theory provides no explanation for why "normal profits" will be different from zero in a long-period analysis, much less what actually determines the "normal" rate of profit, is one of its most glaring deficiencies. Marxists explain capitalist profits as the result of the difference between the amount of "value" labor power creates when used in production – the "use-value" of labor power – and the amount of "value" employers must pay for labor power – the "exchange value" of labor power. Sraffians explain profits as the result of employers expropriating part of the surplus of goods produced in a productive economy from those who produced them. The chapter argues that a "fundamental Sraffian theorem" is a more straightforward explanation for the origin of profits than the "fundamental Marxian theorem," and also avoids a mistaken belief that capitalist profits derive only from the amount of labor they hire, when in fact profits derive from a markup on non-labor as well as labor costs of production.

[margin note: Sounds like Shaikh wouldn't agree – see –]

In chapter 3 the Marxian and Sraffian analyses of technical change are presented and compared. A major flaw in Marxian theory is the prediction that there will be a tendency for the rate of profit to fall as workers are equipped with ever more produced inputs to work with, i.e. that capital deepening, or automation, will lead to crises of profitability. The source of the misconception in Marxian theory is explained, and a logically consistent Sraffian analysis of technical change is presented as an alternative. A bonus to the Sraffian theory of technical change is that it reveals that capitalists cannot be trusted to always adopt more productive technologies and reject less productive technologies – a flaw in capitalism Marxism never identified.

[margin note: certainly weighted labor & materials argument]

Chapter 4 compares Marxian theories of crises with post-Keynesian, neo-Kaleckian, Minskyan, and structualist theories which share a methodological framework with Sraffian microeconomic theory. The chapter explains why Marxian "tendency for the rate of profit to fall" and "under consumption" theories of crisis mislead people into the false belief that capitalism is plagued by "internal contradictions" and will therefore inexorably dig its own grave, distracting attention from genuine sources of crises other heterodox schools of macroeconomics now focus on.

[margin note: Hahnel says capitalism won't dig its own grave]

Chapter 5 explains why the labor theory of value is ill-suited to integrating inputs from the natural environment into our analysis, and shows how Sraffian theory is well suited to this important task. Not only is it easy to integrate rents paid to owners of natural resources into a Sraffian analysis of price and income determination, it turns out that a Sraffian framework facilitates rigorous measurement of environmental throughput and changes in throughput efficiency so that sufficient conditions for environmental sustainability can be derived for a modern, integrated, multi-good economy.

In chapter 6 Marx's "Hegelian" critique of capitalism is contrasted with a more straightforward, moral critique of capitalism consistent with both Sraffian theory and modern egalitarian philosophical theories of distributive justice.

The conclusion briefly summarizes the advantages of replacing formal Marxian economic theory – which after 150 years has not surprisingly become outmoded in a number of respects – with a thoroughly radical, modern version of Sraffian economic theory.

Note

1 See Albert *et al.* (1986) for a critique of historical materialism and a proposal by seven radical authors for how to build upon its strengths while eliminating its weaknesses.

1

PRICES

The Marxian Theory of Prices

At the time Marx studied political economy "classical" economists, most notably Adam Smith and David Ricardo, used a "labor theory of value" to explain prices. So it was only natural for Marx also to base his explanation of prices on the amount of labor time it took to produce different commodities. Adam Smith explained the logic as follows:

> In that early and rude state of society which precedes both the accumulation of stock and the appropriation of land, the proportion between the quantities of labour necessary for acquiring different objects seems to be the only circumstance which can afford any rule for exchanging them for one another. If among a nation of hunters, for example, it usually costs twice the labour to kill a beaver which it does to kill a deer, one beaver should naturally exchange for or be worth two deer. It is natural that what is usually the produce of two days' or two hours' labour, should be worth double of what is usually the produce of one day's or one hour's labour.
>
> *(Smith 1776: Book I, Chapter 6, paragraph 1)*

However, when classical economists initially developed a labor theory of value to explain relative prices they did not have all the mathematical tools at their disposal we have today. Now we know how to systematically calculate the amount of labor time it takes, both directly and indirectly, to produce goods and services in an economy where goods are produced by labor using other produced goods from a description of the technologies being used. Let a(ij) represent the amount of good i required to produce a unit of good j. And let L(j) be the number of hours of "direct" labor required to produce a unit of good j. In a two good economy we might have the following "recipes" for making each good:

a(11) = .3 a(12) = .2
a(21) = .2 a(22) = .4
L(1) = 1.0 L(2) = .5

The first column is the "recipe" being used to make good 1. It takes workers in the industry producing the first good 1 hour working with 0.3 units of good 1 itself and 0.2 units of good 2 to produce 1 unit of good 1. It can help to think of the 1 hour of "direct labor" as the "stirring time" to transform the "ingredients," 0.3 units of good 1 and 0.2 units of good 2, into 1 unit of good 1. The second column is the "recipe" for making good 2. It takes workers in the second industry 0.5 hours working with 0.2 units of good 1 and 0.4 units of good 2 itself to produce 1 unit of good 2. The a(ij)s and L(j)s represent the technology of the economy, which is sometimes convenient to represent as {**A,L**} where the **A** includes all of the a(ij)s and **L** includes all the L(j)s.

Notice we are assuming there is only one "primary" input in production, labor. Everything is ultimately made by labor and labor alone. Yes, to make good 1 we need some of good 1 itself and some of good 2 along with labor – that is what the recipe for making good 1 says. But these inputs of goods 1 and 2 were, in turn, produced by labor. In chapter 5 we consider what happens when some other non-produced input from "nature" is required to produce things along with labor. But for now, we assume labor is the only non-produced input in our economy. Moreover, we also assume labor is "homogeneous." That is, there are not different kinds of labor – carpenters and welders, for example – where production sometimes requires one kind of labor and not the other. Again, we will discuss what happens if we relax this assumption later, but for now we are simply establishing a suitable mathematical framework to represent the thinking of classical economists, including Marx, when they developed the labor theory of value.

Given the above technological data how can we calculate the number of hours it takes not only *directly* to make a unit of good j, that is L(j), but also the number of hours it took to make the amount of good 1 we need and the amount of good 2 we need to make a unit of good 1, referred to as the time it took to make a unit of good 1 *indirectly*?

Define V(j) as the number of hours of labor needed both directly and indirectly to make a unit of j. In other words, define V(1) and V(2) as the answers we are seeking. Now ask: How many hours did it take to make a(ij)? By definition it takes V(i) hours in grand sum total to make 1 unit of good i. So it must take V(i)a(ij) hours to make a(ij) units of good i. We can now write what are called the "value equations" for the economy:

(1) V(1) = L(1) + V(1)a(11) + V(2)a(21)
(2) V(2) = L(2) + V(1)a(12) + V(2)a(22)

The first equation says: The number of hours it takes in grand sum total to make 1 unit of good 1, V(1), equals the hours of direct labor, L(1) (stirring time, if you will) plus the number of hours it took to make a(11) units of good 1, plus the number of hours it took to make a(21) units of good 2 (the time it took to make the ingredients). The second equation says the same for good 2. Since all of the a(ij)s and L(j)s are "givens," i.e. they are simply the description of the technologies being used, {**A,L**}, there are only two unknowns, V(1) and V(2). While we cannot solve equation 1 without knowing the value for V(2), and we cannot solve equation 2 without knowing the value of V(1), we can solve the two equations simultaneously to obtain mutually consistent values for V(1) and V(2).

In this book we will only encounter equations which can be solved as long as there are as many equations as there are unknowns. So counting equations and unknowns will be important. Fortunately in the case of our value equations there are two equations and two unknowns, and we are able to solve for the values of the two unknowns, V(1) and V(2). The important point is that the technological data − all the a(ij)s and L(j)s which we represent by {**A,L**} − are sufficient to calculate the labor values in our economy, the V(j)s, which we can represent by **V**. Symbolically: {**A,L**} → **V**.

Substituting the numerical values above into our value equations gives:

V(1) = 1 + .3V(1) + .2V(2)
V(2) = .5 + .2V(1) + .4V(2)

Which can be solved to give: V(1) = 1.842 and V(2) = 1.447.

So what does the above quotation from Adam Smith imply the price of good 1, p(1), and the price of good 2, p(2), should be? The prediction is that the price of good 1 relative to the price of good 2, p(1)/p(2), should be equal to the value of good 1 relative to the value of good 2, V(1)/V(2), i.e. that prices in our economy should be proportional to the number of hours it took in grand sum total to make each good. Symbolically we write this as **P** ∝ **V** where **P** represents the price system and **V** represents the value system. And in our particular case: V(1)/V(2) = 1.842/1.447 = 1.273, and therefore a unit of good 1 should exchange for 1.273 units of good 2, i.e. p(1)/p(2) should also be equal to 1.273. Notice that our calculation takes into account a complication Smith did not raise in the quotation above: If a beaver hunter needs a trap, which takes someone time to produce, and a deer hunter needs a bow, which takes someone time to produce, we will have taken that into account as well.

Where Marx believed he had surpassed his predecessors was in discovering an explanation for the origin of capitalist profits even when all goods exchange according to the number of hours it takes to make them, both directly and indirectly.[1] Marx argued that what his predecessors had failed to notice was that in the case of one special commodity, labor power, the amount of labor time it takes to produce it, and therefore its exchange value, is less than the value it confers on the goods it produces when used. Marx argued that this was the answer to the mystery of why profits are positive even when capitalists pay the full "value" for all inputs and receive no more than the "value" for their products.

Consider a capitalist producing shirts: He begins with a certain amount of money which he uses to purchase cloth from a capitalist in the textile industry, sewing machines from their manufacturer, and hire "labor power" to work with the sewing machines to turn the cloth into shirts, which he then sells. Assume that everything is bought and sold according to the number of hours it took to make it, both directly and indirectly, that is according to what Marx called its "exchange value." And for convenience, assume a sewing machine lasts only one year. If it took 50 hours (directly and indirectly) to make the sewing machines that is what the shirt capitalist pays for them. If it took 30 hours (directly and indirectly) to make the cloth that is what the shirt capitalist pays for it. And if it took 20 hours to turn the cloth into shirts using the sewing machines, then the shirt capitalist will be able to sell however many shirts were made for 50+30+20 = 100.

But how much will the shirt capitalist have to pay for the 20 hours of labor power he hired? *If the economy is productive it does not take a full hour to*

produce enough wage goods to keep a worker alive and working for an hour.
Therefore, even if the capitalist pays for the 20 hours of labor power
according to their full value – the number of hours (both directly and
indirectly) it took to "produce" them – that will be less than 20 hours.
Suppose, for example, that amount is 15 hours. In this case the shirt capitalist's
costs will be 50+30+15 = 95 when he pays the full value for all inputs,
including labor power. Since his revenues will be 50+30+20 = 100 when
he sells the shirts for their "value," his profits will be 100−95 = 5.

At this point Marx had achieved his two primary goals: (1) He had an
explanation for prices that was very much in line with everyone else's
explanation at the time, namely that relative prices reflect different amounts
of labor time needed, both directly and indirectly, to produce commodities.
And unlike those writing before him (2) Marx had explained the origins of
capitalist profits: Even when commodities sell according to this principle,
even when all commodities sell at their "exchange values," capitalists receive
profits because if the economy is productive it takes less than an hour (both
directly and indirectly) to produce the bundle of wage goods needed to keep
a worker alive and working an hour, i.e. the "exchange value" of labor
power is less than the value labor power imparts when used. *Voila!* We are at
the end of Volume I of *Capital*.[2]

However, there were two problems. (1) It turns out that prices will *not* be
proportional to labor values in capitalism.[3] Moreover, (2) the size of a capitalist's
profits depends on the amount he spends on *all* inputs, not just how much he
spends purchasing labor power, i.e. the size of his wage bill. We take up the first
problem later in this chapter and leave the second problem to chapter 2 where
we discuss profits. But first, let's see how Sraffians explain prices under capitalism.

The Sraffian Theory of Prices

Assume the same two good, two industry economy as before:

$$a(11) = .3 \; a(12) = .2$$
$$a(21) = .2 \; a(22) = .4$$
$$L(1) = \; 1.0 \; L(2) = .5$$

Let $p(i)$ be the price of a unit of good i, w be the hourly wage rate, and $r(i)$
be the rate of profit received by capitalists in sector i. The first step is to
write down an equation for each industry that expresses the truism that
revenue minus cost for the industry is, by definition, equal to industry

profit. If we divide both sides of this equation by the number of units of output the industry produces we get the truism that revenue per unit of output minus cost per unit of output must equal profit per unit of output. Another way of saying this is: cost per unit of output plus profit per unit of output must equal revenue per unit of output. This is the equation we want to write for each industry.

The second step is to write down what cost per unit of output and revenue per unit of output will be for each industry. For industry 1 it takes a(11) units of good 1 itself to make a unit of output of good 1. That will cost p(1)a(11). It also takes a(21) units of good 2 to make a unit of output of good 1. That will cost p(2)a(21). So [p(1)a(11) + p(2)a(21)] are the non-labor costs of making one unit of good 1. Since it takes L(1) hours of labor to make a unit of good 1 and the wage per hour is w, the labor cost of making a unit of good 1 is wL(1). Revenue per unit of output of good 1 is simply p(1).

What is profit per unit of output in industry 1? By definition profits are revenues minus costs, so profits per unit of output must be equal to revenues per unit of output minus cost per unit of output. Also by definition the rate of profit is profits divided by whatever part of costs a capitalist must pay for in advance. Dividing both the numerator and denominator by the number of units of output in industry 1 gives us the truism that the rate of profit in industry 1 is equal to the profit per unit of output in industry 1 divided by whatever part of costs per unit of output capitalists must advance in industry 1. Therefore, the profit per unit of output in industry 1 must be equal to the rate of profit for industry 1 times the cost per unit of output capitalists must advance in industry 1.

Assume that capitalists must pay for all costs in advance.[4] So the cost per unit of output capitalists must advance in industry 1 is [p(1)a(11) + p(2)a(21) + wL(1)]. Also assume that the rate of profit capitalists receive is the same in both industries, r, since otherwise capitalists would move from industries with a lower rate of profit to industries with a higher rate of profit until their profit rates became the same.[5] Therefore:

profit per unit of output in industry 1 = r[p(1)a(11) + p(2)a(21) + wL(1)]

And we are ready to write the accounting identity, or truism, that cost per unit of output plus profit per unit of output equals revenue per unit of output in industry 1:

[p(1)a(11) + p(2)a(21) + wL(1)] + r[p(1)a(11) + p(2)a(21) + wL(1)] = p(1)

Which can be rewritten as: $(1+r)$ $[p(1)a(11) + p(2)a(21) + wL(1)] = p(1)$. Writing a similar equation for industry 2 we get what are called the "price equations" for the economy:

(3) $(1 + r)$ $[p(1)a(11) + p(2)a(21) + wL(1)] = p(1)$
(4) $(1 + r)$ $[p(1)a(12) + p(2)a(22) + wL(2)] = p(2)$

The price equations are 2 equations with 4 unknowns: w, r, p(1), and p(2). (Recall the a(ij) and L(j), i.e. {**A,L**}, are technological "givens.") But we are only interested in *relative* prices, i.e. how many units of one good trade for how many units of another good. If we set the price of good 2 equal to 1, $p(2) = 1$, then p(1) tells us how many units of good 2 one unit of good 1 exchanges for, and w tells us how many units of good 2 a worker can buy with her hourly wage. So we now have 2 equations in 3 unknowns: w, the "real" hourly wage rate, r, the uniform rate of profit in the economy, and p(1), the price of good 1 *relative* to the price of good 2. We do not have as many equations as unknowns, and therefore cannot solve yet for the values of our unknowns.

However, we can ask: What would r and p(1) in this economy be if the wage rate were, for example, $w = 0.691$? In which case we simply substitute $w = 0.691$ and $p(2) = 1$, along with the data representing our technologies (or recipes) for producing the two goods, into the two price equations and solve for p(1) and r. Solving:

$(1 + r)[.3p(1) + .2(1) + 1(.691)] = p(1)$
$(1 + r)[.2p(1) + .4(1) + .5(.691)] = 1$

Gives: $p(1) = 1.273$ and $r = 0$.

And we can ask: What if the conditions of class struggle are such that workers' wage is only 0.500 units of good 2 per hour? What will p(1) and r be? Solving:

$(1 + r)[.3p(1) + .2(1) + 1(.500)] = p(1)$
$(1 + r)[.2p(1) + .4(1) + .5(.500)] = 1$

Gives: $p(1) = 1.190$ and $r = .126$ or 12.6%.

And we can ask: If the conditions of class struggle are such that workers only receive $w = 0.400$, what will p(1) and r be? Solving:

$$(1 + r)[.3p(1) + .2(1) + 1(.400)] = p(1)$$
$$(1 + r)[.2p(1) + .4(1) + .5(.400)] = 1$$

Gives: $p(1) = 1.137$ and $r = .208$ or 20.8%

In our example, as the wage rate falls from 0.691 to 0.500 to 0.400 units of good 2 per hour, the rate of profit rises from 0% to 12.6% to 20.8%. It is possible to prove that this negative relationship always holds, but we leave discussion of how wage rates and the rate of profit are determined according to Sraffian theory to the next chapter. In this chapter we are concerned with explaining prices. In all cases we set $p(2) = 1$, making good 2 what is called our "numeraire," so as explained $p(1)$ represents how many units of good 2 one will get in exchange for a unit of good 1, and w represents how many units of good 2 a worker can buy with her hourly wage. Notice what we have discovered so far:

- As we change from one possible combination of (w, r) to another, that is from (w = 0.691, r = 0.00) to (w = 0.500, r = 0.126) to (w = 0.400, r = 0.208), $p(1)$, the price of good 1 relative to good 2, changes from 1.273 to 1.190 to 1.137 *even though production technologies are the same in all three situations.* Clearly relative prices are not determined by technology alone. Clearly income distribution plays a role in price determination.
- *Only* in the case where r = 0 is $p(1) = 1.273$. So only in the case where r = 0 are relative prices proportional to the labor values of the two goods. Whenever r is different from zero relative prices are no longer proportional to labor values, but deviate systematically from labor values.[6]

Comparing the Marxian and Sraffian Theories of Prices

What at first appears to be a big difference between the two explanations of prices, in fact is not. It appears that the Marxian theory of prices is determinate while the Sraffian theory is not. According to Sraffian theory we cannot determine what relative prices and the rate of profit will be until we know what the wage rate is. On the other hand, in the Marxian system it appears we have an immediate answer to what relative prices and the rate of profit will be without need for more information – even if we have to make some sort of technical adjustment to "transform" labor value prices into "prices of production" to make those prices consistent with equal rates

Hahnel: wage rate determines profits

of profit in all industries, as we will soon discuss. But in fact, both systems are equally determinate, or indeterminate.

To make the Sraffian explanation of relative prices and the rate of profit determinate all one has to do is stipulate a given real wage rate, w. Moreover, the only reason the Marxian theory gives an immediate answer to what prices and the rate of profit will be is that Marx implicitly specified a real wage rate when he assumed that labor power will exchange according to the number of hours it takes (both directly and indirectly) to produce a particular wage bundle, in his case the bundle sufficient to keep a worker alive and working for an hour, i.e. a subsistence real wage. In short, in neither theory is it possible to derive relative prices and the rate of profit until a real wage rate has been stipulated. In both Marxian and Sraffian theory a real wage must be stipulated before relative prices and the rate of profit can be derived.[7]

However, there is a major difference between the Sraffian and Marxian theories of prices under capitalism. Marxian theory starts with technology, derives labor values, and then, as we will soon see, must "transform" these labor values into what Marxists call "prices of production" which are consistent with equal rates of profit in all industries. In other words the process is: $\{\mathbf{A}, \mathbf{L}, w_s\} \rightarrow \mathbf{V} \rightarrow \mathbf{P}$ where w_s stands for a subsistence wage rate. Whereas Sraffian theory derives prices consistent with equal rates of profit in all industries directly from technologies and a given real wage: $\{\mathbf{A}, \mathbf{L}, w_a\} \rightarrow \mathbf{P}$ where w_a stands for any wage rate workers manage to achieve.

First, it is well known that it is possible to go from $\mathbf{V} \rightarrow \mathbf{P}$. It is also well known that Marx's suggestion for how to perform this calculation, i.e. how to "transform values into prices of production" in Chapter IX of Part II of Volume III of *Capital* does not work.[8] But it is also well known that many others, beginning with Ladislaus Bortkiewicz in 1906, have derived algorithms which begin with $\mathbf{V}$ and successfully end up with $\mathbf{P}$. Since $\mathbf{P}$ is a relative price vector while $\mathbf{V}$ is a vector of absolute values, there is one degree of freedom when performing the transformation. This has given rise to many different "solutions" to the transformation problem depending on one's choice of how to turn the relative price system into an absolute price system, i.e. on choice of a numeraire. And much ink has been spilled among Marxist economists debating over which choice of a numeraire is "more consistent" with Marx's argument, or intent, which choice "better illustrates" some valuable lesson about how capitalism functions, etc. But the question is: *Why bother?* If we can derive prices of production directly from technologies for any real wage − as Sraffian theory demonstrates we can – why bother first to calculate labor values, only to have to go to the trouble of deriving a correct set of prices starting from labor values?

I am not the first to ask this question and suggest that we should not go to the extra trouble. Eugene Bohm-Bawerk pointed out in *Karl Marx and the Close of His System* published in 1896, two years after Volume III of *Capital* was published in 1894, that the theory of value from Volume I was redundant since the prices of production Marx derived in Volume III could be correctly determined without reference to labor values. Paul Samuelson made this point in a particularly poignant way:

> I should perhaps explain in the beginning why the words 'so-called transformation problem' appear in the title. As the present survey shows, better descriptive words than 'the transformation problem' would be provided by the 'problem of comparing and contrasting the mutually-exclusive alternatives of "values" and "prices".' For when you cut through the maze of algebra and come to understand what is going on, you discover that the 'transformation algorithm' is precisely of the following form: 'Contemplate two alternative and discordant systems. Write down one. Now transform by taking an eraser and rubbing it out. Then fill in the other one. Voila! You have completed your transformation algorithm.'
>
> *(Samuelson 1971)*

However, before citing Occam's razor and declaring discussion closed because prices under capitalism can be explained without referring to labor values, and are not equal to labor values in any case, we should consider if there is any reason why beginning with labor values on our way to explaining prices might be insightful. Is there something we learn from doing so, something we might otherwise fail to understand? Over the years various Marxist economists have suggested different rationales for defining and using labor values to understand how capitalist economies function. They fall into four categories:

1. In capitalist economies values originate first, and subsequently become transformed into prices. In other words, our intellectual transformation reveals something important about the actual process of price formation in capitalist economies.
2. A transformation from value prices to prices of production occurs when a pre-capitalist market economy Marx called "simple

commodity production" is transformed into a capitalist economy. In other words, our intellectual transformation mirrors a hypothetical, or perhaps an actual historical, transformation, from one kind of economic system to another.

3. Labor values are necessary because otherwise the origin of profits will remain a mystery.
4. Capitalism is best understood by studying production first and exchange second, and values are needed to understand production, while prices of production are only necessary to understand exchange.

We consider the first two rationales here and leave the last two rationales until the next chapter when we compare Marxian and Sraffian theories of profits.[9]

The Transformation Problem

The "transformation problem" is this: If profits come only from the part of financial capital one advances to hire labor power, if capitalists in different industries distribute the portion of the capital they advance between labor power (their wage bill) and produced inputs they purchase from other capitalists (their non-labor costs) differently, and if goods sell at their values; then capitalists in different industries will have different rates of profit.[10] To see this, return to our earlier example, remembering that for convenience we are assuming that machines last for only one year:

Our shirt capitalist advanced 50 for sewing machines + 30 for cloth + 15 for labor power = 95 in total, and he sold the shirts produced by 20 hours of labor power for (50+30+20) = 100, which yielded profits of 5. So the shirt capitalist's *rate* of profit was 5/95 = .05263 = 5.263%.

Now consider a steel capitalist who pays 100 for steel making machines (blast furnaces and rolling mills) because that was the number of hours it took to produce them, both directly and indirectly, 60 for iron ore and coal, because that was the number of hours it took to produce them, both directly and indirectly, and 15 for 20 hours of labor power, which he then puts to work with his machines and ore producing steel. The steel capitalist will be able to sell the steel for 100+60+20 = 180. His cost is 100+60+15 = 175, so his profit is also 5. However, his *rate* of profit is only 5/175 = .02857 = 2.857%. What are we to make of this? There are four possible responses.

(1) The rate of profit in the steel industry will be lower than the rate of profit in the textile industry. Since it is a well-known fact that in the real

world capitalists in different industries do, in fact, often earn different rates of profit, perhaps we have discovered the reason why.

However, all concerned – Marx, Marxians, Sraffa, Sraffians, and mainstream economists alike – all reject this response to our finding. What is agreed by all concerned is that different rates of profit among industries which are not transitory are due to barriers to the mobility of financial capital – because otherwise capitalists would withdraw their financial capital from low profit industries to invest instead in high profit industries until discrepancies in profit rates were eliminated. Moreover, there is no evidence whatsoever that higher rates of profit are correlated with a higher proportion of expenditures on labor compared to non-labor inputs. If anything, higher rates of profit seem empirically to correlate with more capital intensive industries, precisely because they are often characterized by higher barriers to entry.

(2) Clearly the problem arises because steel capitalists only spend $15/175 = .08571 = 8.571\%$ of their financial capital on labor power, i.e. steel capitalists have what Marx called a high "organic composition of capital." While textile capitalists spend $15/95 = 0.15789 = 15.789\%$ of their financial capital on labor power, i.e. textile capitalists have a low organic composition of capital. The second possible response is to conclude that absent barriers to entry capitalists will move their capital from the steel industry (where profits are initially lower) to the textile industry (where profits are initially higher) until the organic compositions of capital become equal in the two industries. Various critics of Marx, including Bohm-Bawerk (1949) and Vilfredo Pareto, have interpreted Marx as suggesting that this is, in fact what happens.

However, most Marxists agree with Ronald Meek (1973) that there is ample evidence that this is *not* what Marx suggested would happen. In any case, there is no reason to believe that if a capitalist moves his financial capital out of steel into textiles this would affect the organic composition of capital in either industry. The organic composition of capital in an industry is determined by whatever is the cost minimizing technology for that industry. When a new capitalist invests financial capital in the textile industry he would presumably invest 15.59% of his financial capital in labor power, just as other textile capitalists do, and capitalists left in the steel industry would continue to invest only 8.571% of their financial capital in labor power.

(3) A third response is that absent barriers to movement financial capital will move from low to high profit industries without changing the organic compositions of capital in either industry, but instead leading to changes in

the prices at which goods sell, i.e. it leads to a modification, or "transformation," of initial labor value prices into "prices of production" which are consistent with a uniform rate of profit in all industries. In other words, rather than affect compositions of capital, the movement of financial capital between industries brings about a change in the prices of the goods they produce which initially sell at their values but then sell at somewhat different "prices of production." As financial capital flows out of steel this raises steel's "price of production" above its labor value so as to increase the rate of profit in the steel industry; and as financial capital flows into textiles it lowers textiles' "price of production" below its labor value to lower the rate of profit in the textile industry. In this interpretation rates of profit become equalized in the two industries by modifications of their selling prices, not by changes in their compositions of capital. At least in the following passage, it seems that this is what Marx had in mind:

> Now if the commodities are sold at their values, then, as we have shown, very different rates of profit arise in the various spheres of production, depending on the different organic composition of the masses of capital invested in them. But capital withdraws from a sphere with a low rate of profit and invades others, which yield a higher profit. Through this incessant outflow and influx, or briefly, through its distribution among the various spheres, which depends on how the rate of profit falls here and rises there, it creates such a ratio of supply to demand that the average profit in the various spheres of production becomes the same, and values are, therefore, converted into prices of production.
>
> (Marx, Capital, Volume III: 195–196)

And it is the interpretation favored by Anwar Shaikh (1977: 134) who argued: "The transformation procedure as set out by Marx reflects the inherent nature of the process of the equalization of profit rates. This is a continuously occurring process, and in its pure form it acts by changing prices of individual commodities while leaving the sum of prices of a given mass of commodities intact."

The problem with this interpretation is there is no evidence of financial capital constantly flowing from capital intensive industries to labor intensive industries to transform labor value prices into prices of production. There is no empirical evidence of any "incessant outflow and influx" and the only reason we need to believe in such a flow is that we started from the assumption that goods initially tend to sell according to their labor values. If we drop the assumption that prices in capitalism tend to be equal to labor values initially we don't need to search for a pattern of financial capital flows that nobody has ever seen.

(4) The fourth possibility is that there is no initial tendency for prices in capitalism to be equal to labor values, i.e. prices in capitalism are *never* equal to labor values. Instead what free mobility of financial capital between industries, or the threat of mobility, does is lead directly to the formation of prices which are systematically different from labor values which yield equal rates of profits in all industries.

Indeed, in other passages Marx himself seems to realize this, even if only in a somewhat confused way:

> As soon as capitalist production reaches a certain level of development, the equalization of the different rates of profit in individual spheres to a general rate of profit no longer proceeds solely through the play of attraction and repulsion, by which market prices attract or repel capital. After average prices, and their corresponding market prices, become stable for a time it reaches the *consciousness* of the individual capitalists that this equalization balances *definite differences*, so that they include these in their mutual calculations. The differences exist in the minds of the capitalists and are taken into account as grounds for compensating. (italics in the original)
>
> *(Marx,* Capital, *Volume III: 209)*

Only if one begins with a belief that some capitalists are prone to have higher profit rates than others because they spend a higher proportion of their financial capital on labor power is there any need to worry about something reaching the "consciousness" of capitalists, or capitalists discovering an equalization to balance "definite differences" – whatever that may mean.

Indeed, the solution is quite simple: Free mobility of financial capital leads directly to the formation of what Marx called prices of production. There is no tendency for labor value prices to form in the first place. In capitalist economies labor value prices do not appear first, and then require transformation into prices of production. Capitalists who spend a higher proportion of their financial capital on labor are not prone to higher rates of profit than those who spend a higher proportion on non-labor inputs. Free mobility of financial capital in a competitive capitalist economy renders all inputs to production equally "exploitable" as evidenced by the ability of all capitalists to mark-up an equal amount on all forms of costs, regardless of whether they are labor costs or non-labor costs. However, this simple, and rather obvious solution is the Sraffian solution, and implies that labor values are redundant, if not misleading, in explaining price formation in capitalism.

But what about the second rationale for studying labor values? Are not labor values necessary in order to understand the difference between price formation in a pre-capitalist market economy and price formation in a competitive capitalist economy? This argument has much more to recommend it. Indeed, one important thing to understand about different economic systems is why they generate different price signals, even if their technologies, resource endowments, and consumer preferences are the same.

As long as we do not attempt to use labor values to explain prices in capitalist economies, there is no reason they may not be helpful in explaining price formation in some other economic system, such as the one Smith alluded to as an "early and rude state of society" and Marx called "simple commodity production." The defining characteristic of such a system is the absence of employers and employees. There are no employers seeking the highest rate of profit available as they hire employees to work with inputs they provide. There are no employees who lack the necessary wherewithal to produce themselves, and who therefore have no choice but to hire themselves out to capitalists for an hourly wage. There are only self-employed producer/consumers who may from time to time exchange commodities with one another.

However, even in such an economy notice there is an implicit assumption that every deer hunter could just as easily (and happily) trap beaver if he so chose; and every beaver trapper could just as easily (and happily) hunt deer if he so chose. Because only then if it takes twice as much time to trap and skin a beaver as kill and dress a deer would no deer hunter ever accept less than 1 beaver pelt for 2 deer, and no beaver trapper accept less than 2 deer for 1 beaver pelt. In sum, labor values may well be a useful way to understand relative prices in some non-capitalist economy under some very stringent and unrealistic assumptions, even if they are not helpful for understanding price formation in capitalist economies.

Notes

1 Like many others, Marx was fully aware that profits sometimes derive from "buying cheap and selling dear." But Marx realized that while this may explain

why a particular capitalist achieved positive profits, it does not explain why capitalist profits would be positive *in general*, or *on average*. And Marx correctly surmised that even if no capitalist ever "bought cheap and sold dear," i.e. that goods always sold at their "values," capitalist profits would be positive.

2 By this I do not mean to imply that people should not bother to read volume 1 of *Capital* – far from it. It is a truly transformative experience I recommend for everyone. Volume I is well worth reading for the historical information it contains about the deplorable working and living conditions endured by the working classes during Britain's industrialization under capitalism, and for the indignation and outrage that leaps from Marx's pen. I am simply saying that the formal model and the conclusions based on it which Marx develops in Volume I reduce to the summary I have provided here.

3 Not only Marx, but before him David Ricardo and even Adam Smith were aware of this problem, which we take up below.

4 When writing the price equations for the economy Sraffa and his followers usually assume that capitalists must pay only for non-labor inputs in advance, and can pay their employees out of the revenue from current sales. However, since we are comparing Sraffian theory with Marxian theory we make the same assumption here as Marx and his followers, namely that capitalists must pay for labor as well as all non-labor inputs in advance.

5 In effect we are assuming there are no barriers to entry or movement of financial capital from one industry to another, and engaging in what Kurz and Salvadori (1995) call "a long-period analysis." Marxians (with a few notable exceptions) and Sraffians both conduct their analysis at this level of abstraction.

6 For proof that these results *always* hold in a more general Sraffian model see theorem 13 in Hahnel 2017.

7 We leave discussion of the similarities and differences between Marxian and Sraffian explanations for the real wage to next chapter. But it is worth noting here a crucial difference between "classical" and "neoclassical" explanations of price and income determination. Both Marxian and Sraffian "classical" explanations of prices and profits require a prior determination of the wage rate. Moreover, in neither of these classical theories is the wage rate determined entirely by the marginal productivity of labor, or the rate of profit determined by the marginal productivity of something called "capital," as they are in neoclassical theory.

8 Anwar Shaikh (1977) demonstrated that while Marx's solution does not work, if we treat Marx's attempt as merely the first step in an iterative process, and do perform the operation Marx did over and over again, we can eventually arrive at the correct prices of production.

9 There is a fifth reason to define labor values which does, indeed, prove useful to understanding one reason capitalist economies cannot be trusted to achieve "dynamic efficiency." However, since Marxists have little interest in whether or not the capitalist price system accurately represents social opportunity costs, ironically this rationale for defining and using labor values is not one Marxists have emphasized. In any case, we will put labor values to good use in chapter 3 when we analyze technological change and "dynamic efficiency" in a Sraffian framework.

10 Paul Sweezy explained the problem as follows: "According to the theory of Volume I, commodities exchange in proportion to the quantity of labor (stored-up

and living) embodied in them. Surplus value (or profit), however, is a function of the quantity of living labor alone. Hence, of two commodities of equal value one with relatively more living labor will contain more surplus value than one with relatively more stored-up labor; and this implies that equal investments of capital will yield different rates of profit depending on whether more or less is put into wages (living labor) on the one hand or material accessories (stored-up labor) on the other. But this theory contradicts the obvious fact that under capitalism equal investments, regardless of their composition, tend to yield equal profits." Introduction to Bohm-Bawerk 1949: xxiii.

2

PROFITS

The Marxian Theory of Profits

As explained in chapter 1, Marx believed he had discovered the answer to the mystery of where profits come from even when capitalists must pay for all inputs according to their labor values and sell their outputs according to their labor values. Marx argued that the answer lies in one special commodity capitalists buy, labor power, which has the unique ability to produce more value when used than the number of hours it takes to produce it, and therefore capitalists have to pay for it. Michio Morishima (1974) provided a formal representation of this explanation of the origin of profits in what became known as the "fundamental Marxian theorem" (FMT).

It is important to understand how the rate of exploitation is defined in Marxian theory. Marx measured labor time in days, but it can also be measured in hours, as is now commonly done by Marxists who have formalized the labor theory of value using linear algebra, and as we have done throughout this book. Using hours as our unit of labor time, Marxists define the "exchange value" of labor power as the number of hours it takes to produce a worker's hourly wage bundle, i.e. the number of hours it takes to "produce" a worker ready and able to work for an hour. So if the real hourly wage bundle consists of $b(1)$ units of good 1 and $b(2)$ units of good 2, and if the labor value of good 1 is $V(1)$ and the labor value of good 2 is $V(2)$, then the number of hours it takes to produce a worker's real hourly wage bundle, and the "exchange value" of labor power, is $V(1)b(1) + V(2)b(2)$. In modern Marxist theory this is represented as **Vb** where **V** is a row vector of labor values and **b** is a column vector of commodities in workers' real hourly wage bundle. And if all commodities sell according to their exchange values, as Marx assumed at this stage of his analysis, this is what employers must pay for an hour of labor power. Marx then observed that the "use value" of labor power to its new owner, the employer, is the number of hours it incorporates into, or "embodies," in the goods produced in an hour, which will determine what the capitalist can sell them for. In sum, the use value of an hour of labor power is 1 hour, while the exchange value of an hour of labor power is the number of hours it takes to produce the worker's wage bundle, **Vb**. The difference between the "use value" of labor power and the "exchange value" of labor power is what Marx called "surplus value," which in modern Marxist notation is $(1-\textbf{Vb})$. Finally, Marx defined the "rate of exploitation" as the ratio of surplus value to exchange value of labor power, i.e. the fraction of each hour the worker is, in effect, working for her employer (her unpaid labor), divided by the fraction of each hour she is, in effect, working for herself (her paid labor.) Or, in modern Marxist notation the *rate of exploitation* is $(1-\textbf{Vb})/\textbf{Vb}$. What Morishima proved in 1974 is that if and only if $(1-\textbf{Vb})/\textbf{Vb} > 0$ will $r > 0$, i.e. that if and only if what Marx defined as his *rate of exploitation* is positive will the rate of profit in the economy be positive.[1] Morishima's FMT is commonly verbalized as: If and only if the rate of exploitation of labor is positive will the rate of profit be positive, i.e. profits come from exploiting labor.

There is no problem with Morishima's proof of the FMT. However, there are four problems with the Marxian explanation of profits as deriving from the exploitation of one input to production, labor power. (1) As in the case of prices, labor values are not necessary to explain profits, i.e. they are redundant. (2) The choice of labor power as the input capitalists "exploit" is arbitrary since any other input can be used to tell the same story. (3) The implication that only one input is an "exploitable" source of profits is misleading because in fact capitalists mark-up on the cost of every input they buy. And finally, (4) belief that profits derive only from exploiting labor can mislead one to think that automation will depress profits, which, as we will see next chapter, it does not. After presenting the Sraffian theory of profits we discuss the first three problems with the Marxian theory in this chapter, leaving the last problem to chapter 3 where we discuss technical change.

[handwritten margin note: The 4 problems w/ Marx's theory of profits already dealt w/]

[handwritten note at bottom: Morishima: profits come from exploiting labor]

The Sraffian Theory of Profits

The Sraffian theory of profits starts with what it means for the economy to be "productive" and its ability to produce a physical economic "surplus." Consider our example of a two sector economy:

a(11) = .3 a(12) = .2
a(21) = .2 a(22) = .4
L(1) = 1.0 L(2) = .5

Notice what happens if we produce one unit of each good. We will use up 0.3 units of good 1 making 1 unit of good 1, and 0.2 units of good 1 making 1 unit of good 2. So in total (adding across the first row) we will use up 0.5 units of good 1, and therefore have 1−0.5 = 0.5 units of good 1 left over as "net output," or surplus, when we produce 1 unit of good 1 and 1 unit of good 2 as "gross output." We will also use up 0.2 units of good 2 making 1 unit of good 1, and 0.4 units of good 2 making 1 unit of good 2. So in total (adding across the second row) we will use up 0.6 units of good 2, and therefore have 1−0.6 = 0.4 units of good 2 left over as "net output," or surplus, when we produce 1 unit of good 1 and 1 unit of good 2 as "gross output." We describe this by saying that our technology is such that the economy is "productive" or capable of producing a physical "surplus." Indeed, Sraffian theory is sometimes referred to as "the surplus approach."

It is clear from our example that if the economy were not productive, if it were incapable of producing a surplus of any good after replacement of all inputs used up, there could be no profits and the rate of profit would necessarily be zero.[2] However, in our case the economy is productive and capable of producing a physical surplus of goods. Does this mean the rate of profit will be positive? That depends on how much of the "surplus" goes to workers as wages, and therefore how much is left over for capitalists as profits.

In our example, to produce 1 unit of good 1 requires 1 hour of labor, and to produce 1 unit of good 2 requires 0.5 hours of labor. So when we apply 1.5 hours of labor to our economy (summing across the third row) to produce 1 unit of gross output of each good we get a surplus of 0.5 units of good 1 and 0.4 units of good 2. If the real wage per hour consists of 0.333[3] units of good 1 and 0.266 units of good 2, the entire surplus of goods produced will go to the workers who produced it. This is because 0.333 units of good 1 per hour times 1.5 hours = 0.5 units of good 1, the entire surplus of good 1, and 0.266 units of good 2 per hour times 1.5 hours = 0.4 units of good 2, the entire surplus of good 2. If the real wage per hour is anything less than this, some of the physical surplus of goods 1 and 2 will go to capitalists and profits will be positive. This result is generalized and proved as theorem 11 in Hahnel 2017. To contrast it with the fundamental Marxian theorem, FMT, I have named it the fundamental Sraffian theorem, FST, which says: If and only if there is a physical surplus of goods after wages have been paid will profits be positive.[4] In other words, if and only if those who produce goods are deprived of some of the surplus goods they produce can capitalists have positive profits.

There is another way to see this which also sheds light on the relationship between the wage rate and the rate of profit in the economy. In chapter 1 we calculated that when the wage is equal to 0.691 units of good 2 per hour, the rate of profit in the economy will be zero. This is because if we apply one hour of labor to the economy in such a way that we produce no surplus of good 1 – that is we produce only enough good 1 to replace all we use up – and we produce all of the economic surplus as a physical surplus of good 2, the surplus will be precisely 0.691 units of good 2.[5] Therefore, if the wage per hour is 0.691 units of good 2, there is no surplus left over for profits, and the rate of profit will be zero. On the other hand, if w falls to 0.500 units of good 2 per hour, then $0.691 - 0.500 = 0.191$ units of good 2 will be left over for profits, which is sufficient to yield a rate of profit of 12.6%. And if w falls to 0.400, then $0.691 - 0.400 = 0.291$ units of good 2 will be left over for profits, which is sufficient to yield a profit rate of 20.8%.

Clearly the fact that the rate of profit rises when the wage rate falls in our example is no accident. The negative relation between the hourly real wage rate and the rate of profit is a well-known result in Sraffian economics, frequently represented graphically as the "wage-profit frontier."[6]

The Sraffa model makes clear that it is the economy that is productive. Or at least it is the entire economy as a whole that is potentially productive, i.e. capable of producing a surplus of physical goods even after all produced inputs are replaced. In fact we might say the framework makes this not just clear, but "crystal clear" to use a phrase made famous by the movie *A Few Good Men*. In other words, the productivity of the economy is a characteristic of the known technologies for producing all goods and services. Of course the economy is only potentially productive, and produces nothing until real people actually go to work and turn this potential into an actual surplus of useful goods and services. So a more careful and accurate wording would be that while it is the economy as a whole that is potentially productive at any point in time, the physical surplus of goods is produced by those who

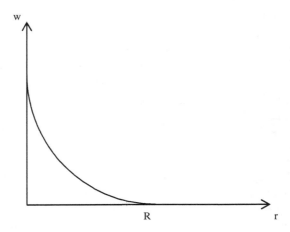

FIGURE 2.1 The wage-profit frontier

work, and thereby realize the economy and their own potentials. Edward Bellamy explained it this way in 1897:

> The main factor in the production of wealth among civilized men is the social organism, the machinery of associated labor and exchange by which hundreds of millions of individuals provide the demand for one another's product and mutually complement one another's labors.... The element in the total industrial product which is due to the social organism is represented by the difference between the value of what one man produces as a worker in connection with the social organization and what he could produce in a condition of isolation.... It is estimated, I believe, that the average daily product of a worker in America today is some fifty dollars. The product of the same man working in isolation would probably be highly estimated on the same basis of calculation if put at a quarter of a dollar.... Now tell me... to whom belongs the social organism, this vast machinery of human association, which enhances some two hundredfold the product of every one's labor?
>
> *(Bellamy 1970: 88)*

Moreover, the productivity of Bellamy's "social organism" has continually increased. Based on research by Richard Sutch, William Nordhaus, Angus *we say workers are more "productive" but where does this additional productivity come from (comparing engineers of today w/ those of 100 years ago)*

Maddison, William Baumol, Nathan Rosenberg, Moses Abramovitz, and others, Gar Alperovitz and Lew Daly summarize the consensus among economic historians: "A person working today the same number of hours as a similar person in 1800 – and working just as hard and no harder – can produce many, many times the economic output. Recent estimates suggest that national output per capita has increased more than twenty fold since 1800. Output per hour worked has increased an estimated fifteen fold since 1870 alone" (Alperovitz and Daly 2008: 3). But if individuals do not really improve, i.e. if individual intelligence and effort change little over time, where does all this increase in productivity come from?

setn: O/L

Robert Solow opened economists' eyes to how little mainstream growth models explain when he estimated that growth in the supply of capital goods and labor explained perhaps as little as 10%, and at most 20% of the growth in US output in the first half of the twentieth century, leaving a "residual" of as much as 80 to 90% – which Solow observed could only be explained by "technical change in the broadest sense." Those who have tried ever since to pin down exactly what is responsible for such a large residual have discovered the extraordinary role knowledge plays in generating economic growth. When <u>Paul Romer</u> searched for an answer to the puzzle that a college educated engineer today is far, far more productive than one working 100 years ago, despite the fact that they each have the same human capital, he concluded that the reason was obvious: "<u>He or she can take advantage of all the additional knowledge accumulated as design problems that were solved during the last 100 years</u>" (Romer 1990: 83–84).

Solow – technical change 80–90%

More broadly, the efficiency of storing and retrieving the scientific, technical, and cultural cumulative knowledge available to each of us has created what Douglas North called the "scaffolding" of economic growth. Moreover, the popular image of this creative process as a sequence of "great inventions" by "extraordinary heroes" appears to be largely a myth. Instead, the process of technological change is most often far more collective, collaborative, and cumulative – diverse contributions slowly build up over time until a breakthrough becomes all but inevitable.

While the Sraffian framework represents it simply as the existing technologies, or recipes available to produce each and every good, {A, L}, it is, of course, much more complicated. {A, L} represent not only the known recipes for making goods and services but also the knowledge and skills necessary to use them, the elaborate divisions of labor they require, and all of the institutions, both formal and informal, necessary for maintaining and coordinating this elaborate division of labor. Moreover, all of this was worked out by countless people, going back over countless years.

Economic historian Joel Mokyr refers to all this productive knowledge as a "gift from Athena," explaining that "technological progress… has provided society… an increase in output that is not commensurate with the increase in effort… necessary to bring it about" (Mokyr 1992: 3). A character in Bellamy's famous utopian novel *Looking Backward* explained it in simple terms to a time traveler from a capitalist past:

> How happened it that your workers were able to produce more than so many savages would have done? Was it not wholly on account of the heritage of the past knowledge and the achievements of the race, the machinery of society, thousands of years in contriving, found by you ready-made to your hand? How did you come to be possessors of this knowledge and this machinery, which represent nine parts to one contributed by yourself to the value of your product? You inherited it, did you not?
>
> *(Bellamy 1960: 100)*

In any case, whatever we call it, the important point is that what allows us to be as productive as we are is something that each generation inherits collectively from all who went before us – irrespective of whether or not some among us appropriate parts of our common inheritance and extract tribute from others before we are permitted to use it.

In case it is not already "crystal clear" that it is the entire economy that is productive, in case it is not "crystal clear" that this is our generation's common inheritance from all generations before us, in case it is not "crystal clear" that any debts which may be owed by some today to others today for this common inheritance are trivial and inconsequential compared to the unpayable debt all today owe to all who preceded us – the Sraffa framework provides a final useful reminder: <u>Although any particular technical change necessarily takes place in some particular industry, how much any technical change increases labor productivity can only be meaningfully measured as an increase in labor productivity in the economy</u> *as a whole*. Which is why how much any technical change increases productivity can be measured by a single number, $p(l)$, the percentage increase in the productivity of the economy *as a whole* which a particular technical change in a particular industry creates.[7]

In conclusion, Sraffians first explain what it means for an economy to be productive and capable of producing a physical surplus of goods. After which the explanation of the origins of profits and the relationship between the wage rate and profit rate are straightforward: (1) Profits result when some of the physical surplus of goods produced in a productive economy is taken away from those who produced it by their employers. (2) The lower the real wage, the more of the surplus is taken away from workers, and therefore the higher the rate of profit will be.

Summary of Sraffian theory of Profits

Comparing Theories of Profits

Marx believed labor values were necessary to explain where profits come from. Sraffians explain where profits come from without reference to labor values. Marxians explain profits as the result of exploiting a unique input to production, labor power. Sraffians explain profits as the result of denying workers in a productive economy all of the surplus goods they produce.

But how can the FMT and FST be reconciled, since they seem to provide different answers to the question of where profits come from? Because both theorems are true it must be the case that if and only if the economy is productive after wages are paid will the rate of exploitation as defined in Marxian theory be positive. And indeed this can be shown to be the case.[8] In other words, just as values proved to be redundant when explaining capitalist prices, the Marxian rate of exploitation proves to be redundant when explaining capitalist profits.

Moreover, we could just as easily define a theory of value based on any basic good in the economy.[9] In fact, one can prove that the rate of profit is positive if and only if *every* basic input is "exploited" when we choose to define values embodied in terms of that input. As John Roemer explained: "One cannot maintain, as is frequently done, that labor power is that one special commodity that mysteriously produces more value than is embodied in it, and hence its exploitation is the sole cause of profits. For, as an alternative to labor value, one could choose corn to denominate value, defining the embodied corn values of all commodities, and the following would be true: The economy is productive in the sense of being capable of producing a surplus if and only if corn is exploited" (Roemer 1981: 52). In which case the verbal statement of Morishima's FMT theorem would be: Profits come from exploiting corn – hardly a ringing call to arms for workers of the world to unite! In short, positive profits have nothing to do with exploitation of one input to production rather than another. The notion

theory of value can be based on any good in economy

All inputs are "exploited" - labor is not special

that there is one *special* input, labor, whose exploitation is the source of capitalist profits is arbitrary since *any* basic input can be chosen to tell the same story.

Moreover, the fact that capitalists obtain profit based on every input to production, not just the labor they hire, is a fundamental characteristic of capitalism, not some sort of deception we must avoid being tricked by, as Marxists would have us believe. Capitalists achieve positive profits by markups on *every input*, not just labor. And it is anyone who does not understand this who is deceived, and fails to understand something important about how capitalism works!

To be clear, there *is* something *qualitatively* unique about labor compared to other inputs. When a capitalist pays for an hour of what Marx called "labor power," what he gets is the right to try and extract an hour of "labor done," but exactly how that will work out is unknown in advance. Whereas, when a capitalist buys non-labor inputs he can be much more sure what using those inputs will accomplish. The struggle between employers and employees over extracting labor from labor power is crucial to many aspects of how capitalism functions, and forms the basis for the very insightful radical "conflict theory" of the firm.[10] However, while labor is qualitatively unique it is not quantitatively unique in the way the Marxian labor theory of value and Morishima's fundamental Marxian theorem imply. An hour of labor done is no different than a ton of steel as far as being "exploitable" and a source of capitalist profits. In fact, one could argue that the traditional Marxist focus on a false *quantitative* distinction between labor done and other inputs to production has sometimes distracted attention from a true *qualitative* distinction between labor power and all other inputs, which does have profound implications.

Instead of searching for an input which is magically capable of "expanding value" during production, it turns out that reality is much simpler: It is the productivity of the economy after wages are paid that allows for positive profits. It is because workers are denied part of the surplus goods they produce that profits are positive. There is no need to elaborate a labor theory of value to make this point; no need to define a complicated technical ratio defined in terms of labor values; and no misleading identification of one input in particular that holds the key to the origins of profit, when in fact every input could be used to tell the same story, and markups on *all* inputs are where profits come from. Sraffian theory identifies the actual surplus of goods workers produce which capitalists manage to expropriate by markups on all inputs they purchase, and establishes a strong *prima facie* case that those

Hahnel: Marxists have been focusing too much on the labor theory of value. Its sufficient to take the Sraffian perspective and say profits come from the production of surplus who do no work, but nonetheless consume part of the physical surplus others produce, are parasites.

Marxian and Sraffian Theories of Wages

Sraffians make clear that they believe the level of the real wage is determined by a host of factors, including political factors, that lie beyond the scope of what a formal economic model or analysis can predict, but can be summarized as "bargaining power," or "class struggle." And in particular, Sraffians point out that the real wage need not be a subsistence wage, as it is implicitly assumed to be in formal Marxian theory. In fact, Sraffians emphasize that the real wage can climb a great deal above subsistence if the economy becomes sufficiently productive and workers gain sufficient bargaining power to keep their employers' rate of profit in check so that increases in labor productivity translate into real wage increases instead of increases in the profit rate.

In truth, both Marx and his followers emphasize the importance of class struggle over the real wage. Nonetheless, in their formal theory the real wage is determined by an assumption having to do with their (provisional) theory of prices, namely that all commodities, including labor power, will exchange according to the number of hours it took to produce them. By doing so Marxian formal theory implicitly treats labor power as if it were produced under similar conditions to other commodities, and therefore, like other commodities will exchange for the amount of time it took to produce it – which in the case of labor power is the amount of time it takes to produce a subsistence wage bundle.

Malthus famously argued that any rise in the real wage above a subsistence level would lead to an increase in birth rates and/or fall in death rates sufficient to push the wage rate back down to subsistence. But Malthus' "iron law of wages" has fallen into disrepute among modern demographers as real wages in the advanced capitalist economies have risen considerably over the past two hundred years. And to be fair, Marx dismissed the Malthusian "iron law of wages" as a "libel against the human race." However, to make reality square with the implicit assumption in their formal theory that labor power is paid a subsistence wage, Marxists have to explain why the "value of labor power" is not simply a matter of biology and counting calories. They must explain how cultural and historical influences affect what the value of labor power will be in any society. <u>Sraffians, on the other hand, take a more direct approach to the real wage</u>: *It's all about bargaining power, stupid!*

Mahnel:
Marxists argue that wages are subsistent (or @ subsistence level)
Sraffians say its about their bargaining power.

Labor Values, Profits, and the Economic Surplus

Last chapter we concluded that labor values were neither necessary nor useful for understanding price formation in capitalist economies. However, it has been argued that even if labor values are not needed to explain capitalist prices, they are needed to understand profits and/or production. We deferred discussion of those rationales for conducting analysis in terms of labor values to this chapter.

Some Marxists argue that labor values are necessary because the origin of profits can only be understood by studying labor values. They argue that without Marx's key insight that the value of labor power is less than the labor time it imparts to goods during production it is impossible to understand where profits come from – except as the result of capitalists "buying cheap and selling dear," which no doubt explains where some capitalists' profits sometimes come from, but does not explain why normal, or average, profit rates for capitalists as a whole are positive. And Marxists cite the FMT as further proof that labor values are needed to explain profits.

However, as we have seen the FST provides a more straightforward explanation of where profits come from, and FST ↔ FMT because in formal terms saying that it takes less than an hour to produce an hourly subsistence wage bundle, $\mathbf{Vb} < 1$, is the same as saying the economy is still productive after wages are paid, $\mathrm{dom}(\mathbf{A}+\mathbf{bL}) < 1$. Moreover, we have also seen that if labor is "exploited" then every other basic input in production is also "exploited" if we define the value of commodities as the amount of that input needed directly and indirectly to produce it. In short, the key to understand profits is that (1) the economy must be productive, i.e. capable of producing a surplus of goods after all goods used up are replaced, and (2) workers must be denied part of the surplus of goods they produce. Moreover, this has nothing to do with labor values or any particular input to production.

Finally, other Marxists argue that capitalism is best understood by studying production first and exchange second, and that values are essential to understanding the former, while prices of production are only needed to understand the latter.[11] It is very important to be clear here: There is a major difference between "classical" economic theory, which begins by focusing on production and the surplus of goods produced after all produced inputs are replaced, and neoclassical theory which does not identify and focus on a physical surplus from production prior to analyzing price and income determination. Both Marxian and Sraffian theories are in the "classical tradition" in the sense that they begin with production of a surplus. So beginning with production, thinking clearly about what it means for an economy to be productive, and recognizing there is a surplus of goods which emerges from production, which then gets distributed among different classes, is extremely important in classical economics, and both Marxian and Sraffian theory proceed in this way.

However, the belief that production can only or best be analyzed in terms of labor values does not follow. It does not follow that to understand why we end up with a surplus of goods as the result of production we must identify where some extra "value" came from. Marxian economics uses the labor theory of value to identify and analyze what happens to the surplus *value* created in production.[12] Sraffian economics identifies and analyzes what happens to the *physical* surplus of goods created in production without resort to labor values. In other words, Sraffian theory simply explains where the extra goods came from. The fact that we can identify and quantitatively measure a physical surplus from production in a multi-good economy without recourse to values demonstrates that values are redundant for identifying the surplus which does, indeed, emerge from the production process.

Unlike neoclassical economists, both Marxians and Sraffians emphasize that aggregate profits are only possible if a surplus is generated in production, i.e. that aggregate profits cannot emerge from the exchange of commodities which merely distributes whatever surplus was already there. The difference is that Marxists claim the surplus that emerges from production after replacing all produced inputs used up and paying workers a subsistence wage, can only be demonstrated and quantitatively measured as a magnitude of "surplus value." Sraffians, on the other hand, emphasize that a "physical surplus" of actual goods emerges from production, show how the magnitude of this physical surplus can be measured rigorously without resort to values, and explain that the price system distributes this physical surplus of goods among capitalists as profits.[13]

For those who recognized that a surplus is generated in production the dilemma was always how to quantify and measure it. In a single good world this is straightforward: Production requires both labor and some amount of a single good in order to produce a larger quantity of the same good. Simply subtract the amount of the good used as an input from the amount of the good produced as output, and you have a quantitative measure of the surplus in physical units of the only good in the economy, which can also be expressed as a fraction of the amount of the good produced. But in a multi-good world, where production requires both labor and specific *how to measure the size of the surplus? Marx says based on labor values — Sraffa produces the "standard commodity"*

quantities of *different* goods in order to produce larger quantities of many different goods, it was never obvious how to measure the size of the surplus. In the nineteenth century the labor theory of value provided a preliminary way to achieve in a multi-good environment what was simple to accomplish in a single good environment. In the twentieth century, first Sraffa, and then Sraffians using the Frobenius–Perron theorem, provided a better solution to what we might think of as the "surplus aggregation problem."[1] Sraffa demonstrated that if different goods were produced in specific proportions which he called the "standard commodity," the amount of every good left over as "surplus" divided by the amount of that good produced would be the same for every good. In other words, for a particular vector of gross outputs we would get the same answer to the question "how large is the surplus" – is it 3%, 5%, or 9%? – no matter which good we used to calculate the answer. Following Sraffa others used the Frobenius–Perron theorem to generalize Sraffa's insight. They noticed that Sraffa's standard commodity was simply the right eigenvector for the input coefficient matrix for the economy including the consumption of workers, $(\mathbf{A}+\mathbf{bL})$, and the dominant eigenvalue for this matrix, dom$(\mathbf{A}+\mathbf{bL})$, represents the fraction of production required to replace all inputs used and pay workers in general. For example, suppose dom$(\mathbf{A}+\mathbf{bL}) = 0.95$. This means that after replacement and wage payments, 0.05 of production is left over, as surplus, to be distributed among capitalists.

Sraffian theory has now demonstrated that values are not necessary to identify and measure the magnitude of the surplus that emerges from production. In other words, we don't need concepts that were initially designed to help understand why goods exchange in particular proportions in market economies – labor values – in order to solve the "surplus aggregation problem" in production. Moreover, as we will see next chapter, thinking in terms of surplus *value* instead of a *physical* surplus of goods can mislead one into drawing false conclusions about the impact of capital-using, labor-saving technological change on the rate of profit.

Notes

1 This is not as obvious as it may appear because as we know, inputs and outputs will not actually sell according to their labor values in capitalism. Instead, they will sell at "prices of production" that equalize profit rates across industries. Nonetheless, what Morishima proved was that if and only if $(1-\mathbf{Vb})/\mathbf{Vb} > 0$ will the uniform rate of profit in the economy, r, be positive.

2 For a thorough discussion of alternative formal definitions of what it means for the economy to be productive and their equivalence, see appendix A in Hahnel

2017. Mainstream economists refer to this condition as the Hawkins-Simon condition. For proof that the economy must be productive in order for there to be any possibility for positive profits see theorem 10 in Hahnel 2017.

3 In the decimal .33$\underline{3}$ underlining the last 3 means that the number "3" which is underlined continues indefinitely. In other words .33$\underline{3}$ means .33333333 ... etc. This convention will be used throughout.

4 Formally: If and only if the dominant eigenvalue of $\mathbf{A}^\star = [\mathbf{A}+\mathbf{bL}] < 1$, i.e., if and only if $\mathbf{A}^\star$ is productive and therefore yields a physical surplus, will profits be positive. $\mathbf{A}$ is the matrix of produced input coefficients, a(ij), $\mathbf{L}$ is the row vector of direct labor input coefficients, l(j), $\mathbf{b}$ is a column vector of the quantities of different goods in the hourly wage bundle, and $\mathbf{A}^\star = [\mathbf{A}+\mathbf{bL}]$ is often referred to as the "socio-technology matrix" for the economy because it is determined by the economy's technology, $\{\mathbf{A}, \mathbf{L}\}$ and also by "sociological" factors which determine the real wage bundle, $\mathbf{b}$.

5 To do this we must distribute the single hour of labor between the two industries precisely so as to generate no surplus in the first industry.

6 See theorem 13 in Hahnel 2017 for proof that the relationship between w and r is necessarily negative.

7 See Hahnel (2016a) for proof that increases in overall labor productivity due to any technological change in any industry can be calculated as $\rho(l) = (1-\beta')$ in a Sraffian framework, where $\beta' = dom(\mathbf{A}'+\tilde{\mathbf{b}}\mathbf{L}')$, the dominant eigenvalue for the economy with the new technology, $\{\mathbf{A}', \mathbf{L}'\}$, and a real wage vector $\tilde{\mathbf{b}}$ that reduces the rate of profit in the *old* economy to zero.

8 Formally, if and only if dom$[\mathbf{A}+\mathbf{bL}] < 1$ will $\mathbf{Vb}$ be less than 1, $(1-\mathbf{Vb}) > 0$, and the rate of exploitation, $(1-\mathbf{Vb})/\mathbf{Vb} > 0$. This result is proved as theorem 22 in Hahnel 2017.

9 One of Sraffa's achievements was to explain that "basic goods" – goods which enter into the production either directly or indirectly of every good – play a different role in the economy than "non-basic" goods. In all the examples in this book all goods are basic. See chapter 1 in Hahnel 2017 for discussion of how the existence of non-basics can affect outcomes.

10 See chapter 8 in Hahnel and Albert 1990 for a rigorous presentation of the conflict theory of the firm and evaluation of many insights it provides.

11 Ira Gerstein (1976) presented this argument when presenting a rationale for why bother to transform from values to prices of production: "The transformation is actually between two theoretical levels of the construction of the economic region of the capitalist mode of production. The first of these levels is *production in itself* (*Capital*, Volume I), [where values prove useful] while the second is the complex unity of production and circulation (*Capital*, Volume III) [where prices of production are necessary]."

12 This is the core argument of the so-called "new interpretation" (NI) school of Marxists for why we should bother with labor values. NI Marxists do not argue that values are necessary to explain prices, but instead refer to the "law of conservation of value" in which value (socially necessary abstract labor time, or SNALT) is created in production and conserved in exchange. Whereas Sraffians simply analyze the surplus from production in physical terms, $\mathbf{y} = \mathbf{x} - \mathbf{Ax} = (\mathbf{I}-\mathbf{A})\mathbf{x}$ is the net output vector, i.e. the physical surplus of each good produced; NI theorists insist on conceptualizing the amount of SNALT embodied in these

goods, **Vy**. Their particular twist is to normalize the price vector – that is convert the relative price vector, **p**, into an absolute price vector, by setting the monetary value of net output, m**py**, equal to the total amount of hours embodied in the net output, **Vy**. This normalization choice means that $1/m = $ **py**/**Vy**, which NI Marxists call the "monetary equivalent of labor time" (MELT). See Dumenil 1980, 1984, Foley 1982, 1986, 2000, and Mohun 1994, 2004. As explained below, because Sraffian theory can identify, quantify, and measure changes in the size of the *physical* surplus even in a multi-good world, none of this is any longer necessary.

13 If there are no barriers to entry and exit among industries eventually prices will adjust until the surplus of goods that emerges from production yields equal rates of profit to capitalists in all industries. If there are barriers, and capitalists cannot move freely among industries, a different set of prices will distribute the surplus of goods from production so as to yield different rates of profits in different industries.

3

TECHNOLOGICAL CHANGE

The Marxian Theory of Technical Change

Marx was well aware of, and even expressed admiration for, the fact that compared to all previous economic systems capitalism had greatly increased the pace of technological change. He assumed that individual capitalists are hard driven to adopt any new technology that lowers their cost of production because this would give them a temporary advantage over their competitors, who, in turn, would be quick to adopt cost-reducing changes for fear of being driven out of business. He also viewed capital-using, labor-saving technical change, i.e. capital deepening, or automation, as a means for capitalists to replenish the ranks of what he called the "reserve army of the unemployed" to keep wages down. However, Marx thought that what was in the interest of individual capitalists temporarily might not necessarily serve their collective interests in the long run.

As we have seen, Marx traced the source of profits to the properties of one input capitalists purchase, labor power, which Marx believed has the unique ability to produce more value when used than the number of hours it takes to produce it. However, when we apply this reasoning to capital-using, labor-saving technical change a problem appears to arise.

Go back to our example from chapter 1 of a capitalist making shirts. When we calculated his rate of profit we found that when his employees work 20 hours making shirts for wages sufficient to purchase a subsistence bundle of goods it takes 15 hours to produce, using sewing machines it took 50 hours to produce and cloth it took 30 hours to produce, and when everything exchanges for the number of hours it took to produce it, his profit rate will be: (50+30+20) minus (50+30+15) all divided by (50+30+15) which gives 5.263%. But what if a shirt capitalist discovers that by equipping his employees with better sewing machines, machines that can sew cloth faster, each employee can turn more cloth into more shirts every hour? If these higher quality sewing machines (which for convenience we continue to assume last only a year) take 60 hours to produce, and if employees, working 20 hours with faster machines can turn cloth it took 40 hours to produce into *twice* as many shirts, what will happen? The cost of making the shirts has risen from (50+30+20) = 100 to (60+40+20) = 120, or 20%. But the number of shirts produced has doubled, i.e. increased by 100%. This means that the cost per shirt using the new technology is less than when using the old technology, and would be adopted by profit maximizing capitalists. However, if everything eventually goes back to selling for the number of hours it took to make it, shirt capitalists' rate of profit will be: $[(60+40+20) - (60+40+15)]/(60+40+15) = 4.348\%$. What are we to make of this? There are two possibilities:

1. One possibility is that this is *not* what happens to the rate of profit when capitalists engage in capital deepening – which was the reaction of most economists after *Capital* was published. Most economists reasoned that if capitalists engage in capital deepening it must be because it increases labor productivity, in which case, if the real wage remains constant it should increase, not decrease, the rate of profit in the economy – and therefore something must be wrong with Marx's theory if it suggests otherwise.[1]

2. The other possibility is that the rate of profit *will* eventually decline as capitalists engage in capital deepening, which is what Marx believed to be the case. In short, Marx stuck with his theory and predicted that such a tendency would eventually manifest itself. This became known as the "tendency for the rate of profit to fall" (TRPF), which is often referred to by Marxists as an "internal contradiction" in capitalism, and is cited by some Marxists as one reason capitalism is prone to crisis, or contains the seeds of its own destruction.

To his credit Marx recognized that if capital deepening increases labor productivity this would change how much profit could be gained by hiring

[handwritten margin notes:] tech change increases in short + labor productivity but it raises value + tendency then rate of profit to fall

[handwritten notes at bottom:] exchange value comes from formation of cartel (we are the only ones who can make this trade) – but if there is competition here also, how can they make more profit than anyone else? Because they own the casino when Las Vegas is booming.

a given amount of labor power because it would decrease the amount of labor time it takes to produce the same real wage bundle of goods, and therefore decrease the "exchange value" of labor power which capitalists must pay. In our example, the amount of time it takes to make the shirts in our subsistence wage bundle is now less than it used to be, and therefore capitalists would only have to pay something less than 15 for 20 hours of labor power. Marx called this effect an increase in the "rate of exploitation," and treated it as "counteracting" the "tendency for the rate of profit to fall" produced by a rise in what he called the "organic composition of capital."

Marx's rate of profit, r(M), based on the assumption that all commodities including labor power exchange according to their labor values, reduces to $r(M) = s'(1-q)$. The "rate of exploitation," s', is the ratio of the fraction of an hour an employee works generating profits for her employer to the fraction of an hour she works for herself so to speak. The "organic composition of capital," q, is the ratio of "constant capital" – expenditures on non-labor inputs purchased from other capitalists according to the total number of hours it took to make them – to "total capital" – expenditures on all inputs, including labor power, all paid for in accord with the total number of hours required to produce them.

From the formula $r(M) = s'(1-q)$ it should be apparent that no matter how much capital deepening might increase q, if it simultaneously increases s' sufficiently it need not reduce Marx's rate of profit. Nonetheless, Marx opined that eventually capitalism would kill the goose laying its golden eggs by reducing the amount capitalists spend hiring labor power relative to buying produced inputs for them to work with from other capitalists.[2]

Some Marxist economists[3] continue to search for evidence that capital deepening is finally lowering the rate of profit in the economy, i.e. for empirical evidence that the "tendency" has finally won out over any "counteracting tendencies." We return to this question after presenting the Sraffian theory of technical change.

The Sraffian Theory of Technical Change

The Sraffian framework is well suited to analyzing if any new technological discoveries will be adopted or rejected by capitalists, as well as the effects of technological changes which are adopted on prices, income distribution, and economic productivity.

exchange value doesn't thrive when things are bad, its only on the upswing of the panarchy. On the way down, its use value. exchange value also comes from marketing – this is the monopoly markup.

Choice of Technique

[handwritten: whether a technology is adopted depends on relative input costs + labor costs]

To know whether capitalists will replace an old technique with a new one, we simply compare the cost of producing a unit of output using the old and new technologies at current prices and the current wage rate. If the new technology lowers production costs it will be adopted, and if not it will be rejected. In this respect Sraffa and Marx made the same assumption about how individual capitalists go about deciding to adopt or reject a new technology, which is also what other economists have always assumed.

For example: Suppose when $r = 0\%$, $w = 0.691$, $p(1) = 1.273$, and $p(2) = 1$ a capitalist in industry 1 discovers the following new capital-using, labor-saving technique:

$$a'(11) = .3$$
$$a'(21) = .3$$
$$L'(1) = .8$$

Will capitalists in industry 1 replace their old technique with this new one? The new technique is capital-using since $a'(21) = 0.3 > 0.2 = a(21)$. But it is labor-saving since $L'(1) = 0.08 < 1.0 = L(1)$. The extra capital raises the private cost of making a unit of good 1 by: $(0.3-0.2)p(2)$ or $(0.3-0.2)(1) = 0.1000$. The labor savings lowers the private cost of making a unit of good 1 by: $(1.0-0.8)w$ or $(0.2)(0.691) = 0.1382$. Which means that under these conditions this new capital-using, labor-saving technology lowers the overall private cost of producing good 1 and would be adopted by a profit maximizing capitalist in industry 1. Moreover, all other capitalists in industry 1 would rush to adopt the new technique as well in order not to be underpriced and outcompeted.

However, this does not mean that the new technique would be adopted under different circumstances. For example, suppose $r = 20.8\%$, $w = 0.400$, $p(1) = 1.137$, and $p(2) = 1$, and suppose capitalists in industry 1 discover the *same* new technique. As before, the extra capital raises the private cost of making a unit of good 1 by: $(0.3-2)p(2)$, or $(0.3-0.2)(1) = 0.1000$. But now the labor savings lowers the private cost of making a unit of good 1 by: $(1-0.08)w$, or $(0.2)(0.400) = 0.0800$, which means that under these conditions the new technique raises rather than lowers the overall private cost of making a unit of good 1, and would not be adopted by profit maximizing capitalists.[4]

Technical Change and Prices

Sraffa (1960) himself clarified how new technologies affect relative prices by distinguishing between *basic goods* which either directly or indirectly enter into the production of all goods, and *non-basic goods* which do not: Sraffa demonstrated that technical changes in a basic industry will necessarily affect the entire relative price system. While technical changes in a non-basic industry will simply lower its own relative price, and the prices of any other non-basics if it should happen to enter into their production. To keep things as simple as possible, we assume throughout that all industries are basic, as both industries are in the example we have been using. And therefore any technical change introduced in any industry will affect the entire relative price structure of the economy.

To continue with the same example, what will happen to relative prices if the original conditions are r = 0, w = 0.691, p(1) = 1.273, and p(2) = 1 and the new technology is adopted by capitalists in industry 1? Writing the new price equations for the economy where the new cost reducing technology is being used by all capitalists in industry 1 we have:

$$(1 + r')[.3p(1)' + .3(1) + .8w'] = p(1)'$$
$$(1 + r')[.2p(1)' + .4(1) + .5w'] = 1$$

As always, before we can calculate relative prices and the rate of profit in the Sraffian model we must stipulate a value for the hourly wage rate. Assume the real wage rate remains the same, i.e. that w' = 0.691. Under this assumption we have:

$$(1 + r')[.3p(1)' + .3(1) + .8(.691)] = p(1)'$$
$$(1 + r')[.2p(1)' + .4(1) + .5(.691)] = 1$$

Which can be solved for: p(1)' = 1.232 and r' = 0.8%. Not surprisingly, once all capitalists in industry 1 are using the new technology the price of good 1 relative to the price of good 2 changes: Now a unit of good 1 exchanges for a little less of good 2: p(1)' = 1.232 < 1.273 = p(1).

Technical Change and Income Distribution

How the introduction of cost reducing technical changes might affect the rate of profit in the economy puzzled political economists for over a hundred years. It long appeared that the answer to this question even in a simple framework where homogeneous labor is the only primary input was very complicated, and quite possibly not definitive. A capitalist in a particular industry would not adopt a new technology unless it was less costly and therefore more profitable than the existing technology in the short-run, i.e. unless it was cost reducing at current prices and the current wage rate. However, once all capitalists in the industry adopt the new, lower-cost technology, absent barriers to entry and exit the entire price system would presumably adjust to eliminate "super profits" in that industry. In which case who could say whether at these new prices, **p'**, the new uniform rate of profit in the economy, r', would turn out to be higher or lower than the old uniform rate of profit, r. In our example it turned out that the new uniform rate of profit is higher: r' = 0.8% > 0.0% = r. But who is to say if this will always be the case? Just because the "counteracting tendencies" outweighed the "tendency for the rate of profit to fall" in this particular example of a capital-using, labor-saving technical change, does not mean they will in every case, or most cases – or at least that is what many Marxist economists thought.

However, in 1961, Nobu Okishio proved a theorem that should have put matters to rest once and for all. Okishio proved that *any* technological change that reduces costs at current prices and the current wage rate, and therefore would be adopted by profit maximizing capitalists, would either raise the uniform rate of profit in the economy, or leave it unchanged as long as the real wage remained constant.[5] In other words, the result in our example is no accident: If the new technology is cost reducing at current prices and the current wage rate, and if the real wage remains the same, the new uniform rate of profit in the economy will either be higher or remain the same, but never be lower. In Marxian terms, Okishio proved that what had always been referred to as "counteracting tendencies" necessarily, and always, must overcome any "tendency" for the rate of profit to fall caused by capital deepening. In short, it turns out that the theory that greedy capitalists pursuing greater profits through automation would thereby witlessly kill the goose laying their golden eggs simply does not fly. To mix metaphors, it was a red herring.[6]

Marheel: rate of exploitation counteracts tendency of rate of profit to fall – and its always more powerful (rate of exploitation)

Technical Change and Labor Productivity

Returning to our example, the remaining question is how technological changes affect productivity. This question did not seem to concern Marx himself, nor most of his followers. Perhaps this is because like many others they assumed that any capital deepening that lowered production costs, and therefore would be adopted, would necessarily increase labor productivity. They also were not terribly interested in criticizing capitalism for its lack of efficiency, concentrating instead on "internal contradictions" leading to "crises" and the fact that labor is "exploited." In any case, it is ironic that this is the one place where labor values can be of help.

In the simple framework we are using if the labor value of every good is lower after a new technology has been adopted by all firms in some industry, this means it takes us fewer hours in grand sum total, i.e. both directly and indirectly, to produce each and every good. <u>In short, if all labor values fall, labor productivity is higher. Conversely if all labor values rise, the new technology has decreased labor productivity.</u> Moreover, we don't have to worry that a technical change in one industry might lower the labor value of some goods but increase the labor value of other goods. In the industry where the change took place the labor value of the good it produces either fell, rose, or remained the same. If it fell and it enters into the production of another good, either directly or indirectly, the value of that good must also fall since there was no change in the input coefficients for the production of that good. If it does not enter into the production of another good, either directly or indirectly, the value of that good will remain the same. Similarly, if the labor value of the good where the technical change was adopted increases, the value of other goods must either increase or remain the same. And of course if the new technology did not change the labor value of the good it produces then no values will change.

So did the technical change we have been discussing in our example increase or decrease labor productivity? In chapter 1 we calculated the labor values for the original technologies in our example to be: $V(1) = 1.843$ and $V(2) = 1.447$. We can now calculate the new labor values after the new technology is adopted by all capitalists in the first industry by solving the new value equations:

$$V(1)' = .3V(1)' + .3V(2)' + .8$$
$$V(2)' = .2V(1)' + .4V(2)' + .5$$

Which yield: $V(1)' = 1.750$ and $V(2)' = 1.417$.

<u>Since both labor values are now smaller than before, the technical change clearly increases labor productivity.</u> However, comparing labor values

before and after any technical change only tells us if labor productivity has increased or decreased. It does not tell us *quantitatively* how much productivity has changed.

Part iii of theorem 18 proved in Hahnel (2017) now provides an easy way to calculate the size of changes in labor productivity in the economy as a whole stemming from any technological change: The size of the change in overall labor productivity is $\rho(l) = (1-ß')$ where ß' is the dominant eigenvalue of the matrix $(\mathbf{A}'+\tilde{\mathbf{b}}\mathbf{L}')$, where $\{\mathbf{A}', \mathbf{L}'\}$ defines the technology for the economy after the technical change is adopted, and $\tilde{\mathbf{b}}$ is an hourly real wage bundle large enough to reduce the rate of profit in the original economy, prior to adoption of the new technology, to zero.

Suppose, for example, we find that ß' equals 0.95. In this case adoption of a new technology will *increase* labor productivity by $\rho(l) = (1.00-0.95) = 0.05$, or 5%. If people next year work the same number of hours as they did this year they will produce 5% more goods. Or, if people next year consume exactly what they consumed this year they could work 5% fewer hours than last year. On the other hand, suppose we find that ß' equals 1.05. In this case labor productivity has *decreased* by $\rho(l) = (1.0-1.05) = -0.05$, or 5%, and people will either produce 5% less goods, or have to work 5% more hours. Returning to our particular example, we discovered in chapter 2 that if workers are paid a real wage bundle of 0.33$\underline{3}$ units of good 1 and 0.26$\underline{6}$ units of good 2 per hour they work, the rate of profit in the economy will initially be zero. This allows us to formulate $(\mathbf{A}'+\tilde{\mathbf{b}}\mathbf{L}')$ and calculate its dominant eigenvalue, which turns out to be 0.984166. Which means that if capitalists in industry 1 adopt the new technology in our example, overall labor productivity will increase by $\rho(l) = (1.00-0.984166) = 0.015834$, or 1.5834%.[7] *illustrating that technical change leads to increase in productivity*

Dynamic Efficiency

We now know that replacing the old recipe for making good 1 with the new one increases labor productivity. We know this because it reduces the labor values of both goods, and because $\rho(l) = + 0.015834$, meaning that labor productivity has *increased* by 1.5834%. We also know that profit maximizing capitalists in industry 1 would adopt this new technology if $p(1) = 1.273$, $w = 0.691$, and $p(2) = 1$, and in so doing would have served the social interest by promoting what we might call dynamic efficiency. But we also know that profit maximizing capitalists in industry 1 would reject this new technology if $p(1) = 1.137$, $w = 0.400$, and $p(2) = 1$. In which case capitalists in industry 1 would obstruct the social interest by rejecting a new technology that increases productivity. What are we to make of this?

Adam Smith actually envisioned _two, not one, invisible hands at work_ in capitalist economies: One invisible hand promotes _static efficiency_, and the other promotes _dynamic efficiency._ Smith not only hypothesized that the micro law of supply and demand would lead competitive capitalist economies to allocate scarce productive resources to the production of different goods and services efficiently at any point in time, i.e. achieve static efficiency; he also believed that competition would drive capitalists to search for and adopt new, more productive technologies thereby raising economic efficiency over time, i.e. achieve dynamic efficiency. Smith assumed that _all_ new technologies that reduce capitalists' costs of production – and _only_ technologies that reduce capitalists' production costs – improve the economy's efficiency. We have just discovered that apparently Smith's second "invisible hand" is imperfect just like his first![8] In some circumstances capitalists will serve the social interest by adopting new technologies that increase productivity, but in some circumstances they will not – they will commit what we might call "sins of omission." It turns out that capitalists will also sometimes commit what we might call "sins of commission." In some circumstances capitalists will serve the social interest by rejecting new technologies that decrease productivity, but in some circumstances they will adopt technologies that lower productivity. How are we to make sense of this?

To solve the puzzle we start with what we know: We now know the new technology in our example made the economy more efficient. We know the new technology was capital-using and labor-saving. And we know capitalists in industry 1 embraced it when the wage rate was 0.691 (and the rate of profit was zero), but rejected it when the wage rate was 0.400 (and the rate of profit was 20.8%). The reason for capitalists' seemingly contradictory behavior is now clear: When the wage rate is higher, the savings in labor costs because the new technology is labor-saving are greater – and great enough to outweigh the increase in non-labor costs because the new technology is capital-using. But when the wage rate is lower, the savings in labor costs are less, and no longer outweigh the increase in non-labor costs. Apparently the price signals $\{p(1), p(2), \text{ and } w\}$ in the economy in the first case lead capitalists to make the socially productive choice to adopt the new, more productive technology, whereas different price signals in the second case lead capitalists to make the socially counterproductive choice to reject the new, more productive technology.

No matter how efficient, or socially productive a new capital-using, labor-saving technology may be, it is clear that if the wage rate is low enough (because the rate of profit is high enough) such an efficient technology will become cost-increasing, rather than cost-reducing, and capitalists will reject it. Similarly, no matter how inefficient, or socially counterproductive a new capital-saving, labor-using technology may be, if the wage rate is low enough (because the rate of profit is high enough) the inefficient technology will become cost-reducing, rather than cost-increasing, and capitalists will embrace it.[9] In other words, Adam Smith's second invisible hand works perfectly when the rate of profit is zero but cannot be relied on when the rate of profit is greater than zero. Moreover, as the rate of profit rises (and consequently the wage rate falls), the likelihood that socially efficient capital-using, labor-saving technologies will be rejected, and the likelihood that socially counterproductive capital-saving, labor-using technologies will be adopted by profit maximizing capitalists increases.

Comparing Analyses of Technical Change

Marxists and Sraffians are in agreement that if and only if a new technology reduces costs of production will profit maximizing capitalists adopt it. Marxists and Sraffians are also in agreement that after a technical change is adopted by all in an industry there will be a general adjustment in relative prices to eliminate super profits in the innovating industry, and once again yield a uniform rate of profit throughout the economy. After which, there is a parting of the ways in the Sraffian and Marxian analyses of technical change.

All Sraffians recognize the validity of the Okishio theorem, which lays to rest any concerns that capital deepening will reduce the rate of profit in the economy if the real wage is held constant. Some Marxist economists persist in futile attempts to resuscitate a "tendency for the rate of profit to fall," which we will address in the next chapter. Marxist economists have been largely uninterested in the effects of technical change on productivity – apparently willing to accept that Adam Smith's second invisible hand does work. Consequently it has fallen to Sraffians to emphasize that capitalists can *not* be trusted to always serve the social interest with regard to adopting and rejecting new technologies. The higher the rate of profit and lower the wage rate, the more likely it becomes that capitalists will commit both sins of omission – fail to adopt capital-using, labor-saving technologies that are more productive – and sins of commission – adopt labor-using, capital-saving technologies even though they are less productive.

... this sounds a lot like an increase in the rate of exploitation to me

Notes

1 As we discover below, the implicit assumption shared by Marx and most economists that technological changes that increase labor productivity always reduce production costs, and technological changes that reduce production costs always increase labor productivity does not hold. But this is a different problem from the one discussed here, which is the effect of capital deepening on the rate of profit in the economy.

2 It is interesting how a simple failure in mathematical reasoning can continue to fuel a misconception. When properly interpreted the formula $r(M) = s'(1-q)$ clearly indicates that even if production were completely automated and therefore q approaches one and $(1-q)$ approaches zero, $r(M)$, Marx's rate of profit, would not have to decline as long as s' increases infinitely – which it could if the number of hours it takes to produce a daily subsistence bundle approaches zero. Yet many TRPF disciples remain convinced that since a rising q displaces ever more labor power from production, and labor power is the sole source of profit, this must eventually depress the rate of profit. Many in the steady-state and de-growth movements make a similar mistake when thinking about the relationship between growth of output produced and growth of environmental throughput. They reason that continued growth of output produced must increase environmental throughput no matter how much we "decouple." But the simple mathematical truth is that as long as the rate of growth of throughput efficiency is as high as the rate of growth of output, throughput will not increase but remain constant. See part 2 in Hahnel 2017.

3 A recent example is Fred Moseley 1991.

4 Astute readers may already be curious about two issues this result raises: (1) Are there circumstances under which the new technology would neither lower nor raise the cost of production? Yes. In this example if w = .500, in which case p(1) = 1.190 and r = 12.6%, it will cost the same amount to produce a unit of good 1 using the new and the old technology. More importantly: (2) Does this new technology increase or decrease economic productivity? If it increases productivity, what are we to make of the fact that in the second circumstance capitalists would reject it? If it decreases productivity, what are we to make of the fact that in the first circumstance capitalists would adopt it? We will shortly address this issue.

5 See Okishio 1961 for the original proof. For a proof accompanied by an explanation of the intuition behind the result, as well as clarification of a little noticed conundrum the Okishio theorem raises, see part 1 in Hahnel 2017. Note that this does not mean the rate of profit might not fall. It simply means if it does fall it must be due to some other cause, such as a rise in the real wage, not because capitalists introduced new capital-using, labor-saving technologies.

6 A number of Marxist economists have attempted to save TRPF theory from the death blow delivered by the Okishio theorem to no avail, as discussed in the next chapter.

7 The components for **A**' are a(11)' = .3, a(12)' = .2, a(21)' = .3, and a(22)' = .4. The components for **b̃L**' are b(1)L(1)' = .33̲(.8) = .26̲, b(1)L(2)' = .33̲(.5) = .16̲, b (2)L(1)' = .26̲(.8) = .213, and b(2)L(2)' = .26̲(.5) = .13̲. Adding corresponding components yields a(11)' + b(1)L(1)' = .566̲, a(1̲2)' + b(1)L̅(2)' = .366̲, a(21)' + b(2) L(1)' = .513̲, and a(22)' + b(2)L(2)' = .533̲. Programs to calculate eigenvalues for

matrices are now available online. I used the Comnuan calculator at http://comnuan.com/cmnn01002/. Entering these four coefficients of our 2×2 matrix into the Comnuan calculator yields a dominant eigenvalue of .984166.

8 Smith's first invisible hand fails whenever there are externalities, i.e. effects on "external parties" to a market exchange. This problem was originally pointed out by Alfred Pigou, who was also the first to propose what are still called "Pigovian" taxes in his honor to correct for inefficiencies caused by external effects. See Hahnel 2007 and 2014b for reasons to believe this problem is far more serious than most mainstream economists are willing to admit.

9 For proof that in a simple Sraffian model if and only if the rate of profit is zero will there be a one-to-one correspondence between technological changes which increase labor productivity and cost reducing technological changes see theorem 4.9 in Roemer 1981. For proof that as the rate of profit rises the likelihood that capitalists will commit ever more sins of omission and sins of commission see theorem 4.10 in Roemer 1981.

4

THEORIES OF CAPITALIST CRISES

Marxian Crisis Theory

In the eighteenth and early nineteenth centuries as political economists struggled to understand how the new economic system which came to be called "capitalism" works, some focused on reasons to believe the system was "self-regulating" and capable of sustaining progress indefinitely. But many prominent political economists writing before Marx worried that the system was prone to crises, and that capitalist "development" would prove to be unsustainable in some way or other. Economics had already been labeled the "dismal science" by the time Marx came on the scene, and not because it was boring, but because so many economists predicted a dismal ending.[1] However, Marx predicted dismal endings for different reasons than Thomas Malthus and David Ricardo before him, and formulated his crisis theory in Hegelian terms as "internal contradictions."

Malthus is most famous for his theory of immiseration due to population growth, but he also worried about "general gluts" – an oversupply of output which exceeds the demand to buy it. In a series of letters between them, Ricardo famously assured Malthus that general gluts could only be fleeting because whatever income some people saved, banks like his own would quickly loan to businesses eager to invest as long as interest rates were free to rise and fall to bring saving and investment into equilibrium. In other words, Ricardo argued that as long as income saved and not spent on consumption was loaned to others who spent it on investment goods, aggregate demand should always be sufficient to buy all that is produced.[2] On the other hand Ricardo's theory of differential rent led him to conclude that as population grew and less fertile lands came under cultivation, food prices and therefore wages would rise, squeezing capitalist profits. Ricardo worried that since wages could not be reduced below some minimum, rising rents of landlords as ever less fertile land came under cultivation would inevitably squeeze the profits of capitalists, leaving them little incentive to continue to invest or ultimately even produce.

Marx dismissed the Malthusian theory of population as "a libel against the human race." And by Marx's time, the application of capitalist technologies to "large landed properties" had increased agricultural productivity per acre sufficiently to reduce concern over the problem that troubled Ricardo. Instead Marx wrote about what he believed were three different causes of crisis in capitalism: (1) He explained that unlike barter exchange among ordinary people, crises are quite possible when capitalists participate in a system of monetized exchange, and that "credit accelerates the violent eruptions"[3] when they occur. (2) He reinforced Malthus' concern about "under consumption" crises and railed against "Say's law," which was assumed by most other economists to prove that general gluts were impossible, or at least temporary and self-correcting, until Keynes convinced many economists otherwise six decades later. (3) He pointed out that during the expansionary phase of business cycles when the "ranks" of what he called the "reserve army of the unemployed" became depleted, workers might temporarily win increases in wage rates and "squeeze" profits. And finally, as explained last chapter, (4) Marx argued there was an "internal contradiction" inherent in the very process of capitalist development itself. Marx hypothesized that when individual capitalists adopt technological changes that improve productivity and lower production costs by equipping their workers with more "capital" to work with, capitalists collectively, and witlessly, generate a "tendency for the rate of profit to fall" because profits derive from exploiting labor, whose wages would come to comprise an ever diminishing portion of total capital outlays. In effect, Marx hypothesized that competition among capitalists to lower production costs by substituting capital for labor would drive them to collectively kill the goose that was laying their golden eggs. Since we began an analysis of TRPF theory last chapter, we consider this version of Marxist crisis theory first.[4]

Tendency for the Rate of Profit to Fall (TRPF) Crises

As explained last chapter, all Sraffians are convinced that the Okishio theorem has adequately demonstrated that the TRPF hypothesis was misguided: Any CU-LS technical changes capitalists would ever adopt will not depress the rate of profit in and of themselves, but do just the opposite. On the other hand, many Marxists have searched for ways to hold onto the TRPF theory. Early attempts to rescue the TRPF theory of crisis from the Okishio theorem include Fine and Harris (1979) and Shaikh (1978a) who argued that while the actual rate of profit may rise when capitalists introduce cost-reducing CU-LS technical changes, as the Okishio theorem proves it must, that the "maximal rate of profit" (when $w = 0$) would fall. However, John Roemer demonstrated that while obviously true that the maximum rate must fall for CU-LS changes when the wage rate is zero, this is irrelevant because it can never prevent the actual rate from rising as long as the change is cost-reducing and any positive real wage remains constant (Roemer 1981: 116–117). Shaikh (1978b) also argued that in a model with fixed capital it was possible for CU-LS, cost-reducing technical changes to lower the rate of profit even if the real wage remained constant. Again, Roemer demonstrated that this was impossible as long as capitalists were profit maximizers by proving a generalization of the Okishio theorem in a model including fixed capital (theorem 5.1 in Roemer 1981: 121), and in an even more general vonNeuman model as well (theorem 5.2 in Roemer 1981: 128). Roemer also explained why an argument of Persky and Alberro (1978) to the effect that the profit rate might fall if new technological changes quickly render earlier investments in fixed capital obsolete, is an example of shifting the goalposts based on an implausible assumption of consistent, and therefore inexplicable, underestimation of the rate of technological change (Roemer 1981: 123–124).

By now a majority of self-declared Marxist economists have conceded that thanks to new mathematical tools unavailable to Marx which made it possible to prove the Okishio theorem, the hypothesis that CU-LS technological changes would act to reduce the rate of profit in and of itself was a red herring. The rate of profit may fall for a variety of reasons, but adoption of CU-LS technological change is simply not among the possible causes. However, there are a few Marxists (Shaikh 2016, Moseley 2017) who continue to search for empirical evidence to support the theory, and one school of obdurate Marxists who argue that a "temporal single system interpretation" (TSSI) of Marx's value theory can rescue the TRPF at a theoretical level.[5] The most outspoken representative of this small TSSI school of Marxist economists, which includes Alan Freeman and Ted McGlone, is Andrew Kliman. What he and his fellow TSSI Marxists propose is an alternative framework of analysis for interpreting what Marx was trying to communicate. In Kliman's words:

> On the standard interpretation, Marx had a simultaneist and dual-system theory: inputs and outputs are valued simultaneously, so input and output prices are necessarily equal, and there are two separate systems of values and prices. According to the temporal single-system interpretation (TSSI) of Marx's theory, however: valuation is temporal, so input and output prices can differ, and values and prices, though quite distinct, are determined interdependently.
>
> *(Kliman 2007: 2)*

Stripped of erudite sounding words, what Kliman acknowledges here is that everyone who is not of the TSSI school – those who adhere to what he calls the "standard interpretation" – assumes *for purposes of analysis* that whatever the going price of something is, that is the price one receives when selling it (in our context as an output), and also the price one pays when buying it (in our context as an input.) Based on this assumption, in the "standard interpretation" Marx erred in volume 3 of *Capital* when transforming values into prices of production – i.e. prices that yield the same rate of profit in all industries – because he inadvertently wrote down equations in which capitalists pay for inputs at one price (their "value" prices), while they sell the same goods as outputs at different prices (their "prices of production"). Although, as many Marxists who adhere to the standard interpretation have demonstrated, there is evidence that Marx himself was aware of this error but considered it to be only a technical problem, amenable to solution, which did not affect the substance of his argument. More to the point, it is easy to "correct" Marx's equations so every good always sells for the same price in every transaction, and still calculate by how much every price of production must deviate from its labor value, as a number of Marxists who adhere to the "standard interpretation" have done.[6] What Kliman asserts, however, is that Marx did not inadvertently err. He actually *meant* for prices of inputs, which are purchased at the beginning of the production period, to be different from prices for those same goods when they are sold as outputs at the end of the production period. We will not speculate here about whether Marx inadvertently erred, or meant for the same good to sell at a different price as an output than as an input. Instead, we will ask which assumption is more appropriate *for purposes of analysis*. But before doing so, notice that the TSSI conclusion that technological change can lead to a fall in the rate of profit derives immediately and solely from the assumption that the same good sells at a different price in different transactions.

Consider a capitalist who uses steel to make steel. If one assumes steel capitalists pay a higher price per ton when they buy steel as an input than they receive when they sell steel as an output, steel capitalists will obviously have a lower rate of profit than if they bought and sold steel at the same price. And if we make this price differential large enough we can make steel capitalists' rate of profit as low as we want! More generally, if one assumes that all capitalists purchase inputs at old, pre-deflation prices, and sell outputs at new, post-deflation prices, one can make the uniform rate of profit in the economy as low as one wishes simply by assuming a sufficiently high rate of price deflation – which is all that TSSI Marxists have shown. No complicated examples and tables are necessary to illustrate this. But why should a ton of steel sell at different prices in the same analysis? Why should we reject the "law of uniform price" which has been a staple of every school of economics from time immemorial for most analytical purposes?

As we know from our analysis of technical change in chapter 3, once a new cost-reducing technology has been adopted by all in an industry, and once the prices of all goods have adjusted to re-equalize the rate of profit in all industries, the new vector of relative prices, **p'**, will be different from the old vector of relative prices, **p**. So technical change will lead to changes in *relative* prices, *eventually*. And this is the reason TSSIers give for believing that not only the price of steel, but the prices of all goods will be constantly changing.

However, prices change only after financial capital has had time to move from industries where profits are lower into industries where new technologies have lowered production costs, creating temporary "super" profits. Moreover, these new prices which take time to emerge are simply new *relative* prices. There is no reason to believe that when capitalists adopt new technologies which increase labor productivity[7] this means that we will have either deflation or inflation of prices in general. No school of economics lists technological change as among the causes of changes in the overall price level.

But for the sake of argument, assume that new technologies are adopted which increase labor productivity (although they may not), and assume this leads to price deflation (although there is no reason to believe it would). *Even if all this occurred it would not mean that capitalists would now sell their outputs for lower prices than they had paid for their inputs, which is the reason the rate of profit might fall according to the TSSI school of Marxism.* Even if the new prices were lower than the old prices, the old prices are the prices back before the new technologies were introduced, and the new prices are the prices after the new technologies are introduced *and* capital has moved among industries to re-equalize the rate of profit everywhere. Which means that the old, higher prices are the prices capitalists paid both for inputs and were paid for outputs back under the old conditions of production. The old higher prices are *not* the prices capitalists pay for inputs now, in the new conditions of production. Instead, the new lower prices for inputs would be the prices capitalists now not only sell their output for, they would also be the prices capitalists pay for inputs they now buy under the new conditions of production. So even if there were deflation due to technical changes, there is no reason to believe it would lower the rate of profit.

Admittedly, there are many implicit assumptions behind all notions of equilibrium in economic theorizing, including the kind of "long period analysis" which all classical economists, including Marx, used for purposes of analysis, and which modern day Sraffians use as well. And because comparative equilibrium analysis does not capture dynamic processes, there is often good reason to supplement, or refine, comparative statics with explicit dynamics. But TSSI Marxists conjure up an implicit dynamic that is completely unrealistic as well as unprecedented: The length of time it takes for the entire price structure to adjust to the introduction of new technologies is much longer than the length of time between when capitalists typically purchase their inputs and sell their outputs. Which is why everyone except TSSI Marxists assumes for purposes of analysis that whether a good is being bought as an input or sold as an output, its price is the same.[8]

Having returned the TRPF theory of capitalist crisis to the dustbin of history, what about Marx's other theories about crises in capitalism? In all other cases, if interpreted as *potentials* for crisis – as theories about situations that can, and do sometimes, arise, which *might* trigger a crisis – Marx's discussion is highly illuminating. Not only was Marx an astute observer of where problems can arise, much of his thinking about these situations has been modeled more rigorously and developed more fully by non-Marxist heterodox schools of economic thought since. In other words, Marx did a great deal to advance a realistic assessment of capitalism as a system which cannot always be relied on to self-equilibrate, and can instead easily embark on paths which merit the label "crisis." However, when cast as *inevitable* tendencies, and described as *internal contradictions* which are inexorable and not amenable to remedy, like the TRPF they have all proved to be misleading.

Money, Credit, and Financial Crisis

It did not take Marx long to get to the subject of money in *Capital*. In Chapter III of Part I in Volume I he explains how monetized exchange, where actors sell one commodity, C(1), for money, M, in order to subsequently purchase a different commodity, C(2), which has a greater use-value for them, creates the possibility of a discrepancy between supply and demand in the aggregate because the act of supplying goods, C(1)−M, is distinct, separate, and prior to the act of demanding goods, M−C(2). While presumably people who initiate the first transaction generally do so only to follow rather quickly with the second transaction, i.e. C(1)−M−C(2) will proceed in orderly fashion, Marx pointed out that it is conceivable that something might prevent some of them from doing so, in which case the demand for goods in the market would fall short of the supply. Marx was certainly correct to point out that in contrast to barter exchange, monetized exchange opens the door to potential discrepancies between demand and supply in the aggregate.

In Part II of *Capital*, which follows immediately and is far more quoted, Marx goes on to explain a second profound truth: Capitalists engage in exchange for an entirely different reason than increasing the use-value of commodities in their possession. Capitalists begin with money, M, with which they purchase commodities, C, only in hopes of selling commodities for an amount of money, M', which exceeds M, i.e. M−C−M' > M represents the logic of capitalist participation in exchange. And if capitalists have reason to believe that M' may not exceed M sufficiently, they may well no longer purchase C, waiting for conditions to improve, and thereby disrupt the orderly process of production and consumption. Pointing out that the likelihood of self-reinforcing, disequilibrating forces in market economies is greatly increased by the motive which guides capitalists' participation in monetized exchange, and that the more the credit system is extended the greater the danger of crisis becomes, is an important antidote to presumptions of automatic self-equilibration by financial markets.[9]

However, having made this important point, Marx quickly moved on to a subject more dear to his heart. After explaining in Chapter V of Part II why aggregate profits cannot be explained by capitalists "buying cheap and selling dear" from one another, he proceeded to argue in Chapter VI that in order for M' to exceed M capitalists must find some special commodity which has the peculiar property that its use will generate a greater value than the value it contains in order for M' to exceed M on a regular basis: $\{M-C(i) \rightarrow C(o)-M'\}$ where $\rightarrow$ indicates that a set of commodities capitalists purchase as inputs, $C(i)$, are transformed *during production* into a different set of commodities which capitalists sell as outputs, $C(o)$. In Marx's words: "Our friend, Moneybags, must be so lucky as to find, within the sphere of circulation, in the market, a commodity, whose use-value possesses the peculiar property of being a source of value, whose actual consumption, therefore, is itself an embodiment of labour, and, consequently, a creation of value. The possessor of money does find on the market such a special commodity in the capacity for labour or labour-power" (Marx 1967a: 167). In other words, as explained in our previous chapter on profits, Marx believed that among all of the inputs capitalists purchase, $C(i)$, only the input labor-power is capable of increasing the value of $C(o)$ above the value of $C(i)$ on a systematic basis, and therefore causing M' to exceed M on average.

There is no reason to repeat arguments from previous chapters why Marx's explanation of the origins of profit – based on what proves to be only a temporary, "working" assumption that all goods, including labor-power, are bought and sold according to their "exchange values" – is less compelling than the Sraffian explanation of where profits come from based on our ability to identify and measure the magnitude of a physical surplus of goods that emerges from production. But there is also no reason to fail to appreciate Marx's argument in the first two chapters of Part II of Volume I of *Capital* that once exchange is monetized, once capitalists motivated by pursuit of profits participate in exchange as major actors, and once money evolves into an elaborate credit system, it would be surprising if financial crises did *not* erupt.

Under Consumption Crises

Rosa Luxemburg expounded on the under consumption version of Marxist crisis theory early in the twentieth century, interpreting imperialism as an attempt to secure more buyers through colonization to stave off stagnation from under consumption in advanced capitalist home economies (Luxemburg 1951). Later in the century Paul Sweezy became the foremost Marxist proponent of an under consumption theory of crisis. Sweezy was thoroughly conversant with previous debates about under consumption crises among

Marxists, which he summarized and evaluated in *Theory of Capitalist Development: Principles of Marxian Political Economy* first published in 1942. In 1966, much to the dismay of many Marxists because they did not use the concept "surplus value," but talked instead simply of an "economic surplus," Sweezy and Paul Baran published *Monopoly Capital: An Essay on the American Economic and Social Order* in which they argued that modern US "monopoly capitalism" was intrinsically prone to stagnation for lack of sufficient aggregate demand, and that a great deal of US government behavior, in particular high military spending accelerating the Cold War, could be understood as attempts to counteract this tendency toward ever greater stagnation.

Among Marxist economists debates often rage over how to interpret Marx on any subject, which aspects of Marx's many theories deserve more or less emphasis, and of relevance here, which of Marx's different theories of capitalist crisis is most compelling in some particular historical period. Sweezy and Baran are widely considered to be the most important Marxists who argue that stagnation, or what was initially referred to as a crisis of over-production or under consumption, is the most insightful and relevant of Marx's crisis theories for modern capitalism.

Much of Baran and Sweezy's analysis of post-WWII US capitalism was indeed insightful. What was *not* helpful was the impression they left readers that stagnation is inevitable and unavoidable as capitalism advances. What more careful modeling has since demonstrated is that no matter how much wage growth may lag increases in labor productivity, and no matter how much capitalists' propensity to consume out of a growing share of national income may fall, the sub-optimal growth path this yields can continue indefinitely. In other words, the presumption of an inevitable breakdown is unwarranted. As discussed below, more rigorous modeling by economists beginning with Steve Marglin (1981) demonstrated that there are a number of possible growth trajectories depending on values of key variables, and as undesirable and unnecessary as "profit-led" regimes like those projected by Baran and Sweezy may be, they do not lead to the kind of total breakdown under consumptionist Marxists project. They simply lead to lower rates of capital utilization, and consequently lower levels of production and income than is technically possible.[10]

Profit Squeeze Crises

Marx initially presented this argument as a theory of how profits might be squeezed by rising wages during the expansionary phase of business cycles when unemployment was reduced and worker bargaining power was temporarily increased. He also cited it as a reason why capitalists might favor capital-using, labor-saving technical change to replenish the ranks of the reserve army of the unemployed, relieve pressure to increase wages, and revive profits. In the 1970s a number of radical economists (including me) scoured data over a number of business cycles in the US for empirical evidence that a profit squeeze, or an under consumption, or a TRPF theory of crisis was more consistent with the historical record.[11] Both Marxian and Sraffian economists later developed a long-run version of a profit squeeze theory of crisis as well. And indeed this is one area where there is a great deal of agreement between Marxian and Sraffian economists today: While the expansionary phase of a business cycle can reduce unemployment and increase labor's bargaining power in the short-run, it is also possible that the bargaining power of labor might increase in the long-run as well: Labor-friendly governments, higher levels of unionization, more ample social welfare programs, or simply an increase in worker consciousness might squeeze profits independent of short-run fluctuations in unemployment. A staple of Sraffian theory is that *all* points on an economy's wage-profit frontier are technically possible; and that *where* on the curve any economy will end up is largely determined by precisely the kind of social/political conditions analysts study as potential causes of a squeeze on profits that last longer than the expansion of a typical business cycle. Some Sraffians and Marxians have extended this logic to how an increase in the rents of natural resource owners might squeeze profits just as a secular rise in wages can. Which brings us to our final school of Marxian crisis theory.

Social Structures of Accumulation

Terrence McDonough describes Social Structure of Accumulation (SSA) theory as follows:

> Social Structure of Accumulation (SSA) theory is a theory of stages of capitalism. Capitalist stage theory focuses on periods intermediate in length between a short-run business cycle and overall capitalist history. These periods consist of a long period of relatively stable capitalist accumulation followed by a relatively long period of crisis and break-down. Each of the periods of accumulation is underpinned by a set of institutions designated as an SSA.
>
> *(McDonough, chapter 34: 370 in McDonough et al. 2014)*

The SSA school arose in the United States in the 1970s as what was sometimes called the post-WWII "golden age of capitalism" came to an end, and the "stagflation crisis" emerged in many of the advanced economies.[12] The original authors, who self-identified at the time as Marxists, included Sam Bowles, David Gordon, Thomas Weisskopf, Michael Reich, and Rick Edwards. They were later joined by others including David Kotz, Terrence McDonough, Martin Wolfson, and Phillip O'Hara. Over the past four decades some of the original authors ceased to self-identify as Marxist, and some of the newcomers self-identified as institutionalist or post-Keynesian. Nonetheless, SSA came to be known as a new Marxian approach to crisis theory that differed from older Marxian schools of thought, as explained by McDonough:

> Marxist theories of capitalist crisis had tended to locate crisis in fundamental tendencies of the capitalist economy which were always potentially present. These tendencies included the tendency of the rate of profit to fall, disproportionalities among economic sectors and a tendency for either overproduction or underconsumption. Thus the emergence of crisis would be the present expression of these long-run secular tendencies. The new theories that arose in the 1970s and early 1980s in the wake of the stagflationary crisis did not share the same emphasis on these tendencies. Crises could arise due to the breakdown of the institutional framework which conditioned the previous period of capitalist expansion.... This argument defined recurring crisis periods as more serious than downward fluctuations of the ordinary business cycle, but not as the expression of an ultimate crisis of capitalism.
> *(McDonough, chapter 34: 371 in McDonough et al. 2014)*

Thus, SSA theory is less deterministic than earlier Marxist crisis theories, and in that regard shares more in common with post-Keynesian, neo-Kaleckian, and structuralist heterodox schools of macroeconomics, as discussed below. Many of its authors have provided insightful analyses of different periods of economic history identifying problems which became more severe over decades, and eventually gave rise to new institutional structures, or SSAs, which once again facilitated a revival of profits and accumulation.[13] However, one can question if beyond a great deal of insightful historical analysis – in this case written by economists with greater expertise in economic theory than historians often have – there is an underlying *theory* in the usual sense of the word. Two key "assertions" which can be interpreted as the basis of

SSA "theory" are: (1) If anything comes to threaten the ability of capitalists to receive an acceptable rate of profit, there will eventually be crisis, and a search for some institutional way to revive profits will be launched. And (2) if anything threatens a healthy rate of accumulation (presumably of capital stock), there will be crisis, and a search for some way to revive accumulation will ensue.[14]

In the case of a low rate of profit it is obvious why a crisis would eventually arise. Moreover, we can identify an important economic agent – capitalists – who would press for changes, or a "new SSA" to rectify what is clearly a problem for them. The second proposition may at first seem equally obvious, and seems to be considered equally obvious by most SSA theorists. But is this really the case? What if a high rate of profit were somehow maintained, but accumulation stagnated?[15] Would this trigger a crisis? And who would propel the search for a new SSA to revive accumulation? One can speculate that when accumulation stagnates output may stagnate as well, which means little improvement in living standards for workers, who might press for changes. Or, one can speculate that if accumulation stagnates in one capitalist country that country will lose out in competition – either economic or military – with other capitalist countries where accumulation is more robust. In which case nationalist or military forces might press for a new SSA to revive accumulation. But unlike the case of low profits, the connection between stagnant accumulation and both a crisis trigger and some powerful agents to propel a search for a new SSA is less obvious.

Sraffian Crisis Theory

When Marx wrote economists made no distinction between microeconomic and macroeconomic theory. But in the aftermath of the Great Depression and the "Keynesian revolution," economists agreed to a rough division of labor: Microeconomic theory was to focus on how *relative* prices of *different* goods and services, and the *real* values of *various* distributive variables are determined in private enterprise, market economies. Whereas macroeconomic theory was to focus on determinants of *overall* production and growth of output, *overall* employment, and price inflation or deflation – including how the monetary system might affect *real*, and not merely *nominal*, values of variables. Microeconomists were also far more likely to conduct their analysis under the assumption that actors had "perfect information" and markets were successfully equilibrate, whereas some macroeconomists focused on disequilibrating forces that might prove self-reinforcing and the problem of unknowable uncertainties about the future. In this context, post-WWII crisis theory became part of macroeconomics. And in this context it would seem that Sraffian economics, which is firmly rooted in heterodox *micro*economic theory, has no counterpart to Marxian theories of crisis.[16]

However, this is not entirely the case. If we consider economists such as Michal Kalecki, Joan Robinson, Nicholas Kaldor, Don Harris, Steve Marglin, Lance Taylor, Paul Davidson, Hyman Minsky, Amitava Dutt, Tom Palley, Wynne Godley, Sydney Weintraub, Michael Hudson, Jan Kregel, Geoff Harcourt, Marc Lavoie, Alfred Eichner, Randall Wray, Paul Auerbach, Peter Skott, and Robert Blecker, we have a heterodox school of macroeconomics intellectually allied and linked with Sraffian microeconomics which we can compare to Marxian crisis theory. The important link between Sraffian micro theory and these heterodox macroeconomists, who call themselves post-Keynesian, neo-Kaleckian,[17] and "structuralists," is that they both focus on production of a physical surplus and its distribution, and seek to elaborate theoretical models where definitive conclusions can be deduced from assumptions about the values of key parameters. The division of labor between these heterodox macro theorists and Sraffian micro theorists is based on (1) whether output is broken down into different goods and services or aggregated, i.e. whether analysis is conducted in a multi-good or single good framework, (2) whether analysis focuses on a long-run steady state, or on various possible growth paths, (3) whether uncertainty is a major consideration, and (4) whether money is treated as only a numeraire, or the credit system plays an important role in the analysis. Since this book is about Marx and Sraffa, only a brief description of various schools of heterodox macroeconomics which are *allied* with Sraffian heterodox microeconomic theory is offered here.

Free Market Finance is an Accident Waiting to Happen

The most important modern elaboration of Marx's early warnings that money and credit contain the seeds of crisis is Hyman Minsky's "financial instability hypothesis" (Minsky 1986, 1992). Minsky provides a set of plausible hypotheses about the likely behavior of banks and borrowers and explains how they logically lead to a step by step increase in systemic financial fragility. While he makes no attempt to predict when a "Minsky moment" will arrive, he emphasizes that competent regulation of the financial sector is necessary to avoid such an outcome. In short, post-Keynesian monetary theory and theories of financial crisis are very much in tune with Marx's early warnings, while providing more rigorous analysis.

Say's Law Inverted

According to "Say's Law" in the aggregate production, or supply, creates its own demand. According to what we might call Keynes' "macro law of supply and demand" in the aggregate production, or supply, will follow demand if it can. These two "opposite" visions, perspectives, or hypotheses if you will, give rise to immense differences between competing macroeconomic theories today, and in particular between post-Keynesian and "new classical" theories – the name given to rational expectations, neoclassical, macroeconomic theories. In particular heterodox macro theorists insist on the efficacy of fiscal and monetary stimulus to increase aggregate demand temporarily when necessary, while new classical theorists, like their pre-Keynesian classical counterparts, once again claim, against all evidence, that such efforts are pointless. But as mentioned above, Marx provided a perfectly sound rebuttal to Say's Law long before Keynes was born. So once again, we find that Marx, Keynes, and post-Keynesians are on the same page regarding the possibility of crises due to a temporary lack of sufficient aggregate demand. The difference is that Keynesians explain how fiscal and monetary policy can, and should, be used to address short-run deficiencies of aggregate demand, and post-Keynesians demonstrate how wage-led regimes are both possible and preferable to profit-led regimes in the long-run. In effect, Keynesians and post-Keynesians demonstrate how it is possible to save capitalism from itself, while as we have seen, under consumption Marxists insist that there is a long-run stagnation problem that will eventually prove immune to stop-gap measures to ward it off.

Long-run Growth Trajectories

Which leads us to the most important difference between Marxian and post-Keynesian, neo-Kaleckian, and structuralist theories: They come to different conclusions about what economic growth can look like in the long-run. Non-Marxist theories of "distribution and growth": (1) provide more analytically rigorous explanations for different *possible* growth paths than Marx and his followers; (2) make clear that depending on the values of key variables, both "wage-led" and "profit-led" regimes are possible; (3) emphasize that while failure to achieve full-capacity growth is possible, this need not lead to a total breakdown; (4) establish that there are no "inherent, internal contradictions" that will inevitably bring any capitalist system crashing to an end; and finally, and perhaps most importantly, (5) demonstrate how, when crises do occur, there are various government policy options which can, if used appropriately, "save the day." In contrast, Marxist crisis theories have traditionally projected inevitable collapse, and even social structure of accumulation theory projects the necessity of major institutional changes when any historic structure of accumulation reaches a crisis point.

We have seen how every attempt to salvage TRPF crisis theory from the dustbin of history has proved futile. What has been suggested here — although admittedly not demonstrated — is that theoretically rigorous neo-Kaleckian models of distribution and growth now demonstrate that while stagnation due to low capacity utilization is one possibility, (1) it is not the only possibility, and (2) even this trajectory is economically "sustainable" and need not lead capitalism to "self-destruct." And what has also been suggested is that one of the two key assumptions made by SSA theory, namely that if accumulation slows sufficiently something must give, has been lacking sufficient supporting argument. None of which is to say that completely understandable and justifiable dissatisfaction and disgust with a profit-led, low-capacity utilization, under performing capitalist regime may not lead workers to replace it with a far superior wage-led, full-capacity, capitalist regime — or better yet, with an entirely different and superior system of participatory, ecological socialism.

Notes

1 Scholars attribute the phrase to Thomas Carlyle who described political economy as "dreary, desolate, and indeed quite abject... what we might call... the dismal science." Irrespective of what "dismal" result Carlyle was actually complaining about in this remark, the phrase was soon interpreted as referring to the fact that many political economists predicted dire outcomes.
2 What Ricardo and other devotees of what came to be known as "Say's Law" failed to consider is the possibility that even if all savings are success-fully loaned out, if they are used to purchase assets rather than newly pro-duced investment goods, supply may well fail to "create its own demand" in the aggregate.
3 Marx 1967c: 441. See Chapter XXVII, "The Role of Credit in Capitalist Production."
4 See Weisskopf (1992) for an excellent exposition of Marx's different theories of crisis and their modern champions.
5 See Kliman 1996, 1997, 2001, and 2007, Kliman and McGlone 1988 and 1999, and Kliman and Potts 2015.

6 It is even possible to demonstrate that if one interprets Marx's own transformation (Marx 1867c: 163–164) as simply the first step in an iterative process of updating input prices to conform to the previous output prices until there is no longer any discrepancy, one can achieve a "correct" transformation of values into prices of production. See Shaikh 1977.

7 And as we have seen, just because a new technology is adopted does not mean it necessarily increases labor productivity. When $r > 0$ capitalists sometimes commit "sins of commission" and adopt new technologies which lower labor productivity.

8 It is also possible that TSSI Marxists simply do not understand the role that the law of uniform price plays in economic analysis, and therefore do not understand when it is appropriate. Of course in the real world the same good often sells for different prices in different transactions which take place at the same time. But what it means to have a market for a good, or say that a market is "well ordered," is that arbitrage will reduce real world price discrepancies between different transactions for a given good which take place very close to the same time. In any case, many have published compelling critiques of the TSSI school. For examples see Laibman 2000, Skillman 2001, Mongiovi 2002, Mohun 2003, and Veneziani 2004.

9 When *Capital* was published the vast majority of economists were still convinced by Ricardo's arguments that Say's Law holds. Having failed to heed Marx's argument to the contrary, it took the economics profession another sixty years – and countless recessions and several major depressions – to finally discover the error of their ways with the help of Keynes' *General Theory of Employment, Interest and Money* and the Great Depression of the 1930s.

10 To see that these are the predictable consequences of repressing wages and increasing capitalists' propensity to save in a formal political economy growth model see Hahnel 2014a: 251–259. Theoretical advances in growth theory by heterodox neo-Kaleckians and structuralists during the last decades of the twentieth century, as discussed below, made it possible to determine what the logical consequences of tendencies like those above really are.

11 See Glyn and Sutcliff 1972, Boddy and Crotty 1974, Weisskopf 1979, and Hahnel and Sherman 1982.

12 At roughly the same time a related school of Marxism arose in France. The founding document of the "French Regulation school" was Michel Aglietta's *A Theory of Capitalist Regulation* published in 1979.

13 Classic SSA publications include: Bowles *et al.* 1983, 1986, and 1989, Gordon *et al.* 1982, Kotz *et al.* 1994, McDonough *et al.* 2010 and 2014, and Kotz 2015.

14 McDonough, chapter 34: 372 in McDonough *et al.* 2014.

15 If one responds that this is impossible – that high profits cannot be maintained absent robust accumulation – then SSA theory has only one proposition: healthy rates of profit must be maintained, or a search for a new SSA to revive them will ensue. But one might argue that this is obvious to pretty much anyone, and hardly qualifies as a "theory."

16 Although Sraffa and Luigi Pasinetti are frequently mentioned as among the founders of the "European" school of post-Keynesian economics.

17 While Keynes and his *General Theory* was the inspiration for many who call themselves post-Keynesians, Michal Kalecki and his *Theory of Economic Dynamics* was the inspiration for other heterodox macroeconomists often called neo-Kaleckians.

5

ECONOMY AND ENVIRONMENT

Marxism and the Environment

The labor theory of value is ill-suited to incorporating inputs from the natural environment into either a theory of capitalist prices or a theory of social opportunity costs. But to blame Marx for this would be gratuitous. Marx inherited the labor theory of value from "classical economists" such as Adam Smith and David Ricardo, and like them, Marx lived in a world where there was only one person for every five people alive today, nature's "services" still appeared to be bounteous, and the costs to society of using inputs from nature consisted mostly of the time needed to find and extract them. Besides a few passages where he condemns capitalism for exploiting and despoiling nature as well as workers, what little Marx had to say about inputs from nature appears mostly in Part VI at the very end of Volume III of *Capital*. However, Marx's discussion of "differential" and "ground" rent there differs little from the theory of rent Ricardo had elaborated before him.

But that was then, and now is now. Not only has population grown five-fold since Marx lived, human impact per capita on the natural environment has increased even more. Today a number of essential ecosystems are seriously imperiled, and we are perhaps less than a decade away from triggering cataclysmic climate change.

Lacking a formal framework that facilitates accounting for inputs from the natural environment and focuses entirely on how much labor time it takes to produce things, some Marxists today have scoured Marx's voluminous writings to find a few passages where he conjectured that capitalism would cause what they have labeled a "metabolic rift" between humanity and nature, and treat environmental problems as one of the "crises" that inevitably plague capitalist economies.[1] Citing the master himself – "Accumulate, accumulate! That is Moses and the prophets!" (Marx 1967a: 595) – these "ecological Marxists" argue that because capitalism is all about accelerating economic growth it must be incompatible with environmental sustainability, as if this were obvious.

As discussed in chapter 4, prior to the 1990s Marxists argued that "accumulate, accumulate" leads to what they called "internal contradictions" that render capitalist growth *economically* unsustainable. Some argued that capital deepening would eliminate the source of profits. Others argued that when wage increases failed to keep pace with increases in labor productivity, and capitalists' propensity to save increased, crises would result when aggregate supply outstripped demand. However, more recently ecological Marxists have argued that an even bigger problem arises when capitalism *does* sustain economic growth sufficiently to surpass critical environmental thresholds and become *environmentally* unsustainable. Six American Marxists who have written extensively on capitalism and the environment are David Harvey (1996), James O'Connor (1998), Joel Kovel (2002), John Bellamy Foster (1994, 2000, 2002, 2009), Paul Burkett (2006), and Jason Moore (2015).

In a recent example, John Bellamy Foster and Fred Magdoff (2010) begin their essay "What Every Environmentalist Needs to Know About Capitalism" with an excellent summary of evidence suggesting that we are experiencing a "planetary ecological crisis." They begin a subsequent section titled "Capitalism is a System that Must Continually Expand" as follows: "No-growth capitalism is an oxymoron.... Capitalism's basic driving force and its whole reason for existence is the amassing of profits and wealth through the accumulation (savings and investment) process. It recognizes no limits to its own self-expansion." Foster and Magdoff go on to assert that because capitalism recognizes no limits to its self-expansion, environmental crises can only worsen unless capitalism is replaced by socialism. Before examining whether this argument holds up under scrutiny, or simply assumes its conclusion, let's see what Sraffian theory has to offer.

Sraffian Theory and the Environment

One of the convenient properties of the Sraffian framework is how easily it allows us to incorporate inputs from nature in production and rents paid to their owners into our theory of income and price determination. Suppose in addition to labor and produced inputs production requires a "primary" input from nature. All we need to do is add its input coefficient to our "recipes" for production. Suppose 0.3 units of nature must be present to produce a unit of good 1, 0.2 units of nature must be present to produce 1 unit of good 2, u is the rent per unit of nature, and capitalists must pay for all inputs – produced inputs, labor, and nature – in advance. Now our recipes look like this:

a(11) = .3 a(12) = .2
a(21) = .2 a(22) = .4
L(1) = 1.0 L(2) = .5
N(1) = .3 N(2) = .2

And our price equations look like this:

(5) $(1+r)[p(1)a(11)+p(2)a(21)+wL(1)+uN(1)] = p(1)$
(6) $(1+r)[p(1)a(12)+p(2)a(22)+wL(2)+uN(2)] = p(2)$

Substituting in values for the coefficients and setting p(2) equal to 1 we have:

$(1+r)[.3p(1) + .2p(2) + 1.0w + .3u)] = p(1)$
$(1+r)[.2p(1) + .4p(2) + .5w + .2u] = 1$

The four unknowns we need to solve for are p(1), w, r, and u. If we set two of the distributive variables equal to zero, we can solve for p(1) and the maximum possible value of the other distributive variable. Doing this we find:

w(max) = .691 and p(1) = 1.273 when r = u = 0
r(max) = .798 and p(1) = .781 when w = u = 0
u(max) = 1.900 and p(1) = 1.100 when w = r = 0

We can also discover what the effect of increasing the value of any distributive variable is on the other distributive variables. Suppose, for example, instead of setting w = u = 0 we increase w to 0.100, keep u = 0 and solve for r. We find that r falls from its maximum value, 0.798, when both of the other distributive variables are zero, to 0.584. Also if we raise r from zero to 0.100 and keep w = 0 we discover that u falls from its maximum of 1.9 to 1.485.

In short, integrating rent for primary inputs from nature along with wages and profits as distributive variables poses no difficulties for a Sraffian determination of income distribution and prices. For proof that there is a negative relationship between *all* distributive variables, just as there was in the system with only the two distributive variables, w and r, and that this negative relationship holds even when we expand the system to account for multiple different "primary" inputs from nature, such as iron ore, oil, and fresh water, in addition to land of different qualities, each with its own rental rate, as well as multiple different kinds of labor, such as welding, carpentry, and computer programming labor, each with its own wage rate, see theorem 19 in chapter 1 of Hahnel (2017).

Recently it has also been demonstrated how the Sraffian framework can help establish rigorous sufficient conditions for environmental sustainability.[2] Ecological economists provide the key concept which they call *environmental throughput*. Throughput is material matter from the natural environment's stocks of "natural resources" used up in production processes, and material matter released into "environmental sinks" by human economic activity which diminish their remaining storage capacities.

Some components of environmental throughput are already so large that they threaten to exhaust a crucial "environmental service." For example, scientists tell us if annual global greenhouse gas emissions do not decrease by 80% or more by 2050 we run an unacceptable risk of triggering cataclysmic climate change. Present levels of other kinds of throughput have reached the point where if they increase further they will threaten some key environmental service. Global fresh water throughput may have reached this level. Present levels of other kinds of throughput are still sustainable, either because they do not exceed the regenerative capacity of the natural resource, or because at present levels of throughput the natural resource would still remain abundant for a very, very long time.

Some ecological economists have called for giving up on the goal of increasing production, and instead focusing on achieving a *steady-state*, i.e. zero economic growth, to prevent further growth of throughput. Others in the *de-growth* movement go even further and insist that production must decrease in order to save the environment. But is it true that we must stop increasing production of goods in order to stop throughput from increasing? Or is it possible to produce more goods without increasing throughput? Fortunately, the Sraffian framework allows us to model both production of diverse goods and throughput rigorously so we can become clear when growth of output is compatible with sustainable levels of throughput and when it is not.

But first it is important to notice that the appropriate coefficients for inputs from the natural environment when deriving prices, wages, and rents are not always the appropriate coefficients when measuring throughput. For example, suppose the input from the natural environment is land, measured in acres, and suppose that after a farmer uses the land it remains in exactly the same condition as it was initially. The farmer may well pay rent to a landowner to use the land even though it does not diminish in size, or by hypothesis deteriorate in any way. In which case, in our example if the farmer produces one unit of good 1 on this land she will need to have 0.3 acres available and will have to pay 0.3u in rent. But notice that in this case throughput is zero by hypothesis. On the other hand suppose the input from the natural environment is fresh water drawn from an aquifer. In this case the farmer will diminish the aquifer by 0.3 gallons when she produces a unit of good 1. So in this case water throughput is 0.3 gallons. When calculating environmental throughput we need the coefficients in our production technologies to represent the amount a stock of a natural resource, or the storage capacity of a natural sink, is diminished, which may sometimes correspond with the amount which must be on hand and available for use, but in some cases, as just explained, may not.[3]

To make this distinction we will use the letter T to represent input coefficients for throughput from the natural environment, whereas we use the letter N to represent the quantity of a primary resource from nature that must be on hand. For simplicity we begin by assuming that nature is "homogeneous," i.e. there is only one input from "nature," just as we often begin by abstracting from differences between carpentry, welding, and computer programming labor and assume labor is homogeneous.[4] Suppose our production technologies, which now have throughput consequences, are those below:

$$a(11) = .3 \quad a(12) = .2$$
$$a(21) = .2 \quad a(22) = .4$$
$$L(1) \ = 1.0 \quad L(2) = .5$$
$$T(1) = .2 \quad T(2) \ = .1$$

We can calculate the amount of nature throughput used up, both directly and indirectly, when we produce a unit of each good in exactly the same way we calculated how many hours of labor it takes, both directly and indirectly, to produce a unit of each good. In short, we must account for the fact that to produce a unit of good 1, for example, it also requires some throughput to produce the a(11) and a(21) we need, just as we took into account that it requires some labor to produce a(11) and a(21) when we calculated the labor value, V(1). Define H(1) as the amount of throughput used, both directly and indirectly, when we produce a unit of good 1, and H(2) similarly. Our "throughput equations" are:

(7) H(1) = H(1)a(11) + H(2)a(21) + T(1)
(8) H(2) = H(1)a(12) + H(2)a(22) + T(2)

Substituting in the coefficients in our example:

H(1) = .3H(1) + .2H(2) + .2
H(2) = .2H(1) + .4H(2) + .1

Which can be solved to give H(1) = 0.368 and H(2) = 0.289, the amounts of throughput from the environment "used up" both directly and indirectly when we produce one unit of output of good 1 and good 2 respectively. And if during a year we produce x(1) units of good 1 and x(2) units of good 2, environmental throughput will be: H(1)x(1) + H(2)x(2).

For simplicity assume that the number of units of nature used up by production during some initial year is exactly equal to the number of units which regenerate naturally each year. If the labor force does not grow, and the number of hours worked in each industry does not change, output and throughput will remain constant, throughput will continue to equal regeneration year after year, and the economy will continue to be environmentally sustainable. But what if we discover and adopt new technologies which increase labor productivity?

This will increase economic wellbeing because we will get more goods for the same amount of work, but it will also increase output and therefore environmental throughput. In this scenario the only way the economy can remain environmentally sustainable is if technological change also increases throughput efficiency. In other words, if the 'x's in our above expression for annual throughput increase because of increases in labor productivity, the 'H's in the expression must decrease to the same extent to preserve sustainability.[5]

But we can be even more precise. In chapter 3 we discovered it is possible to rigorously measure the rate of increase of overall labor productivity from any technical change in any industry in a Sraffian framework. It is also possible to rigorously measure the rate of increase of overall throughput efficiency from any technological change in any industry. Theorem 20 proved in Hahnel (2017) provides a way to calculate the size of the change in overall throughput efficiency stemming from any technological change in any industry. The change in throughput efficiency is: $\rho(n) = (1-\alpha')$, where the initial technology for the economy is defined by $\{\mathbf{A}, \mathbf{T}\}$, the technology for the economy after some technical change is defined by $\{\mathbf{A'}, \mathbf{T'}\}$, $\tilde{\mathbf{d}}$ is chosen so $\text{dom}[\mathbf{A}+\tilde{\mathbf{d}}\mathbf{T}] = \alpha = 1$, and $\alpha' = \text{dom}[\mathbf{A'}+\tilde{\mathbf{d}}\mathbf{T'}]$.

Which means that for any technological change, in any industry, we can calculate both how much it changes labor productivity, $\rho(l)$, and how much it changes throughput efficiency, $\rho(n)$. As long as all technical changes introduced in the economy during a year collectively increase throughput efficiency, $\rho(n)$, by as much as they increase labor productivity, $\rho(l)$, environmental throughput will remain constant. Which means that $\Sigma(i) \; \rho(n)(i) \geq \Sigma(i)\rho(l)(i)$ is a sufficient condition for preventing environmental throughput from growing, which in turn means:

*Even if we continue to work the same number of hours from year to year, i.e. we take none of any increase in labor productivity in the form of leisure, it is possible to increase labor productivity and economic wellbeing without putting greater strain on the environment **as long as throughput efficiency grows as fast as labor productivity**.*

Let's see how this works out in the example we have been using. In chapter 3 we analyzed a particular CU-LS technical change in industry 1 which increased labor productivity by $\rho(l) = (1.00-0.984166) = .015834$, or 1.5834%. While it may seem that this change has nothing to do with throughput efficiency, unfortunately this is not the case. Even though the change does not affect $T(1)$, because it increases $a(21)$ it will have the unfortunate effect of increasing $H(1)$, which will indirectly increase $H(2)$ as well. The expression $\rho(n) = (1-\alpha')$ allows us to calculate the decrease in throughput efficiency for the economy as a whole caused by the CU-LS change in industry 1 in our example. In this case it turns out that when $a(21)$ is increased from 0.2 to 0.3, $\alpha' = 1.0419$, and therefore $\rho(n) = -0.0419$, indicating that while the CU-LS change adopted by capitalists in industry 1 increases labor productivity by 1.5834% it also has the unfortunate effect of simultaneously decreasing throughput efficiency by 4.19%.[6]

To prevent putting more pressure on the environment we would need some other technical changes that increase throughput efficiency. Such changes could take place in any industry, but let's explore a single capital-using, nature-saving (CU-NS) change in industry 2 which increases throughput efficiency.

$$a(12)' = .2$$
$$a(22)' = .41$$
$$L(2)' = .5$$
$$T(2)' = .01$$

Notice that such a change in industry 2 will necessarily decrease labor productivity somewhat because it is capital-using. So, as in the case of the CU–LS change in industry 1, we will have to calculate both $\rho(n)$ and $\rho(l)$ for this CU–NS change in industry 2 if we want to know its effects on labor productivity as well as throughput efficiency.

Since our primary focus is on how much this change in industry 2 increases throughput efficiency we calculate this effect first, using the formula $\rho(n) = (1-\alpha')$, and find that $\alpha' = 0.8632$, $\rho(n) = 0.1368$, and therefore this change increases throughput efficiency by 13.68%.[7] But since this change is CU, and therefore adversely affects labor productivity, we must also calculate $\rho(l) = (1-\beta')$ for this change in industry 2. We find that $\beta' = 1.0044$, $\rho(l) = -0.0044$, and therefore this change decreases labor productivity by 0.44%.[8] We have now calculated both effects, of both technical changes – the first a CU–LS change in industry 1 which increased labor productivity but decreased throughput efficiency, and the second a CU–NS change in industry 2 which increased throughput efficiency but decreased labor productivity.

Since $\Sigma(i)\ \rho(l)(i) = + .015834 - .0044 = .011434 > 0$, the effect of the two changes combined increases labor productivity by 1.1434%.

Since $\Sigma(i)\ \rho(n)(i) = - .0419 + .1368 = .0949 > 0$, the effect of the two changes combined increases throughput efficiency by 9.49%.[9]

Since $\Sigma(i)\ \rho(n)(i) = .094900 > .011434 = \Sigma\rho(l)$ the overall increase in throughput efficiency is greater than the overall increase in labor productivity, and therefore annual environmental throughput would be *reduced* if both changes were adopted.

To summarize:

- A change in a labor coefficient only affects overall labor productivity (and not throughput efficiency), and a change in a throughput coefficient only affects overall throughput efficiency (and not labor productivity). However, any change in a capital coefficient will change *both* labor and throughput efficiency, as is apparent from inspection of the equations for labor values, 'V's, and throughput "values," 'H's.[10]

- Therefore, any technical change that changes a capital input coefficient will affect both labor productivity, $\rho(l)$, and throughput efficiency, $\rho(n)$, and a full evaluation of its effects requires calculating both.
- When multiple technical changes are introduced during a year all we need to do is: (1) sum their individual $\rho(l)s$ to calculate the economy's overall change in labor productivity, (2) sum their individual $\rho(n)s$ to calculate the economy's overall change in throughput efficiency, and finally (3) compare $\Sigma(i)\ \rho(n)(i)$ with $\Sigma(i)\ \rho(l)(i)$ to determine whether environmental throughput has increased, decreased, or remained constant.

Comparing Sraffian and Marxian Environmental Theory

Let's return to: "Accumulate, accumulate! That is Moses and the prophets!" What Marx was intent on conveying in this phrase, and for that matter in the whole of section 3, Chapter XXIV, Part VII of Volume I of *Capital* where it appears, is that competition forces capitalists to be relentless accumulators, as no organizers of production before them. But what exactly was it that Marx claimed capitalists are so hard-driven to accumulate? The very next sentence gives his answer: "Therefore, save, save, i.e., reconvert the greatest possible portion of surplus-value ... into capital!" (Marx 1967a: 595). So it is *surplus value* Marx insisted capitalists are driven to "accumulate, accumulate." But surplus value – which is measured in some unit of labor time – is not the same as the physical mass of goods produced – which is measured in appropriate units of weight and volume.

Marx defined surplus value as the difference between the number of hours of labor needed to produce all goods and services minus the number of hours needed to produce the intermediate goods used up in the production process and the consumption goods purchased by the workers with their wages. In other words, the accumulation Marx referred to above is an accumulation of *hours* of labor expended, which he called exchange value, and the growth of surplus value is limited only by the total number of hours worked, and how many of those hours capitalists can manage to appropriate. To be precise, Marx's argument was that competition would drive capitalists to seek to accumulate an ever larger percentage of exchange value as surplus value. In theory, this percentage could continue to increase indefinitely up to 100%,[11] but in any case, it is in no way limited by the availability of physical matter. So just because the planet has physical limits does not mean that capitalist accumulation of surplus value cannot increase indefinitely. And conversely, even if capitalist accumulation of surplus value approached

100% of total exchange value, this implies nothing about breaching physical planetary limits.

In conclusion, the latest version of "inevitable collapse Marxism" by a group of "ecological Marxists" who claim that environmental disaster is unavoidable unless capitalism is replaced by eco-socialism because a continual increase in the growth of capitalist accumulation *of surplus value* is impossible on a finite planet does not survive the sniff test. Those who make this claim fail to realize that value is not throughput, carelessly applying reasoning to value as if it were throughput, and, in effect, are guilty of assuming their conclusion.

As Sraffian theory demonstrates, if hours worked in every industry remain constant, environmental sustainability reduces to whether or not increases in throughput efficiency keep pace with increases in labor productivity, or, as environmental economists put it, on whether or not we can sufficiently "de-couple" growth of output from growth of throughput. It is easy to motivate the impression that this is impossible – that when output of goods increases environmentally damaging throughput must increase as well – by pointing out that this has, in fact, historically been the case under capitalism to date. But that is (a) obvious to anyone who recognizes that we have been exhausting the environment, but (b) completely irrelevant to whether or not this must necessarily continue to be the case.[12] What is at dispute is whether or not throughput efficiency can grow indefinitely. Because if it can, no matter how slowly, then labor productivity, and the increases in economic wellbeing this increase in output of goods brings, can also grow indefinitely at that same rate without any increase in environmental throughput, as has now been proved using a Sraffian framework.

Nothing said here should be interpreted as denying that there is an unhealthy and environmentally destructive growth imperative in today's capitalist economies, and perhaps in any capitalist economy. It just means we must go beyond facile arguments which, upon inspection, prove not to be compelling, to explain why this is the case.[13]

Notes

1 The passage giving rise to a whole school of "ecological Marxism" appears at the very end of section V, "Metayage [share cropping] and Peasant Proprietorship of Land Parcels," in Chapter XLVII, "Genesis of Capitalist Ground-Rent," in Part VI, "Transformation of Surplus Profit into Ground Rent," in Volume III of *Capital*: "On the other hand, large landed property reduces the agricultural population to a constantly falling minimum, and confronts it with a constantly

growing industrial population crowded together in large cities. It thereby creates the conditions which cause an irreparable break ['rift' in some translations] in the coherence of social interchange prescribed by the natural laws of life. As a result the vitality of the soil is squandered, and this prodigality is carried by commerce far beyond the borders of a particular state.... Large-scale industry and large-scale mechanized agriculture work together. If originally distinguished by the fact that the former lays waste and destroys principally labour-power, hence the natural force of human beings, whereas the latter more directly exhausts the natural vitality of the soil, they join hands in the further course of development in that the industrial system in the country-side also enervates the labourers, and industry and commerce on their part supply agriculture with the means for exhausting the soil" (Marx 1967c: 813). Marx also commented on how nineteenth-century "modern" agriculture was destroying soil fertility in section 10, "Modern Industry and Agriculture," in Chapter XV, "Machinery and Modern Industry," in Part IV, "Production of Surplus Value," in Volume I of *Capital*. "Capitalist production, by collecting the population in great centres, and causing an ever-increasing preponderance of town population, on the one hand concentrates the historical motive force of society; on the other hand, it disturbs the circulation of matter between man and the soil, i.e. prevents the return to the soil of its elements consumed by man in the form of food and clothing; it therefore violates the conditions necessary for the lasting fertility of the soil.... Moreover, all progress in capitalist agriculture is a progress in the art, not only of robbing the labourer, but of robbing the soil; all progress in increasing the fertility of the soil for a given time is a progress toward ruining the lasting sources of that fertility.... Capitalist production, therefore, develops technology, and the combining together of various processes into a social whole, only by sapping the original sources of all wealth – the soil and the labourer" (Marx 1967a: 505–506). Whether or not Marx's observations about the deterioration of soil fertility based largely on the work of a nineteenth-century German agricultural chemist named Justus von Liebig can be extrapolated into a compelling theory of how and why capitalism must irreparably destroy the natural environment, as a new generation of "ecological Marxists" claim, is what we examine in this chapter.

2 See chapter 2 in Hahnel 2017 for a more extensive treatment, including proofs of key theorems.

3 In truth what we care about is how much any environmental service deteriorates when goods are produced, but it is common to think of this in terms of diminishing scarce stocks of natural resources or depleting the storage capacity of environmental sinks.

4 See chapter 2 in Hahnel 2017 for discussion of what we can still conclude about sustainability even when nature is heterogeneous, and even when some components of nature do not regenerate.

5 Another way to think about increases in labor productivity is as decreases in labor values, 'V's. If we think about increases in throughput efficiency as decreases in throughput "values," 'H's, then if hours worked remain constant, as long as the 'H's are shrinking as fast as the 'V's, throughput will remain unchanged.

6 In our example a "real rent" consumption vector for owners of nature that would reduce the initial rate of profit to zero even when wages are zero is 1.66

units of good 1 and 1.3̲3̲ units of good 2. Using this to formulate our 2×2 matrix [**A'**+ **dT**] yields: a(11)' + d(1)T(1) = .3 + (1.6̲6̲)(.2) = .6333, a(12)' + d(1)T(2) = .2 + (1.6̲6̲)(.1) = .366̲6̲, a(21)' + d(2)T(1) = .3 + (1.3̲3̲)(.2) = .566̲6̲, and a(22)' + d(2)T(2̲) = .4 + (1.3̲3̲)T(.1) = .533̲3̲. Entering these four coefficients of our 2×2 matrix in the Comnuan calculator at http://comnuan.com/cm nn01002/ yields a dominant eigenvalue of 1.0419, which gives $\rho(n) = -.0419$.

7 Again, in our example a "real rent" consumption vector for owners of nature that would reduce the initial rate of profit to zero even when wages are zero is 1.6̲6̲ units of good 1 and 1.3̲3̲ units of good 2. Using this to formulate our 2×2 matrix [**A'**+ **dT'**] yields: a(11̲)' + d(1)T(1̲)' = .3 + (1.6̲6̲)(.2) = .6333, a(12)' + d(1)T(2)' = .2 + (1.6̲6̲)(.01) = .216̲6̲, a(21)' + d(2)T(1)' = .2 + (1.3̲3̲)(.2̲) = .466̲6̲, and a(22)' + d(2)T(2) = .41 + (1.3̲3̲)(.01) = .423̲3̲. Entering these four coefficients of our 2×2 matrix in the Comnuan calculator at http://comnuan.com/cm nn01002/ yields a dominant eigenvalue of .8632, which gives $\rho(n) = +.1368$.

8 In our example a real hourly wage of .3̲3̲ units of good 1 and .26̲6̲ units of good 2 would reduce the initial rate of profit to zero even when rent is zero. Using this to formulate our 2×2 matrix [**A'**+**bL'**] yields: a(11)' + b(1)L(1) = .3 + (.3̲3̲)(1) = .633̲3̲, a(12)' + b(1)L(2) = .2 + (.3̲3̲)(.5) = .366̲6̲, a(21)' + b(2)L(1) = .2 + (.26̲6̲)(1) = .466̲6̲, and a(22)' + b(2)L(2) = .41 + (.26̲6̲)(.5) = 543̲3̲. Entering these four coefficients of our 2×2 matrix in the Comnuan calculator at http://comnuan.com/cmnn01002/ yields a dominant eigenvalue of $\beta' = 1.0044$ and $\rho(n) = -.0044$.

9 We can confirm the conclusion that in combination the *two* changes – our CU-LS change in industry 1, and our CU-NS change in industry 2 – increase both labor productivity and environmental throughput efficiency by calculating the new labor values and throughput "values" for the new coefficients in both industries and comparing them to the original values before either change was introduced. The new labor values are V(1)' = 1.762 which is less than the original V(1) = 1.842, and V(2)' = 1.445 which is less than V(2) = 1.447. The new throughput "values" are H(1)' = .343 which is less than H(1) = .368, and H(2)' = .133 which is less than H(1) = .289.

10 From the perspective of the environment a CU-LS change must increase throughput because it is CU without being NS. From the perspective of labor productivity a CU-NS change must reduce labor productivity because it is CU without being LS. In effect CU-LS changes substitute more nature for less labor, while CU-NS changes substitute more labor for less nature.

11 Whether or not Marx was correct in anticipating that capitalists would necessarily succeed in appropriating an ever larger share of exchange value is also questionable. If labor's bargaining power did not deteriorate there is no reason to believe this prediction would prove true. But this is beside the point, since even if capitalists' share of total exchange value approached 100%, the conclusion that environmental throughput must necessarily increase does not follow.

12 Take GHG emissions for example: For the period from 1960 to 2000 real global GDP grew at 2.7% per year but global GHG emissions grew only at 1.3% per year *because GHG throughput efficiency increased by 1.4% per year*. However, what scientists are telling us is that unless GHG throughput falls dramatically, i.e. unless increases in GHG throughput efficiency outstrip increases in real GDP considerably, we are headed for climate disaster by mid-century. Which is why

the fact that global GHG throughput efficiency only increased by 0.7% from 2000 to 2014 is worrisome, but the fact that it has started to rise again in the past few years is somewhat encouraging. Nonetheless, increasing GHG throughput efficiency is clearly possible. And if we can increase it enough it is perfectly consistent with continued increases in global GDP. We just need much, much greater increases in GHG throughput efficiency. We need a crash program to reduce fossil fuels in the energy mix and increase energy efficiency.

13 See Hahnel 2013 for discussion of specific ways in which capitalism tends to generate an unhealthy and environmentally unsustainable "growth imperative."

6

MORAL CRITIQUE OF CAPITALISM

Karl Marx was neither the first, nor the last, critic of capitalism. However, he is by far the greatest critic of capitalism. Marx left no doubt that in his opinion an economy where private ownership of the means of production was abolished, workers managed themselves, and the "anarchy" of markets was replaced by democratic planning, was a far superior way for humans to organize our economic activities – even if he wrote precious little about the specifics of how a "socialist," much less a "communist" economy might function. However, Marx was trained in the Hegelian philosophical tradition in which social criticism is presented very differently from how arguments are structured in twenty-first-century moral philosophy. Consequently his "critique" of capitalism was not presented as a moral criticism, and consequently, is anything but straightforward for most who discuss distributive justice today.

For example: Marx pointed out that in general workers *do* receive the full "value" of the labor power they sell according to his theory, even though he argued that only if the rate of exploitation of labor was positive can the rate of profit be positive. Marx famously chastised Proudhon for arguing that "property is theft." Marx often belittled "utopian socialists" for making a moral, rather than a "scientific," critique of capitalism. And Marx did much to make social scientists aware of the fact that what people consider to be fair or unfair is greatly influenced by the economic system in which they live. In short, Marx's methodology rejected any clear distinction

Marx chastizes Proudhon for saying "Property is theft"

between "positive" and "normative" theory, and kept him from making what people today would consider straightforward moral arguments about economic justice and injustice.

Piero Sraffa, and most prominent Sraffians who have further developed the theory he pioneered, have confined themselves to "positive" economic theory and eschewed "normative" theory. Sraffians have been largely content to let readers draw their own conclusions about whether income distribution under capitalism is just or unjust. For example, in 2012 the *Cambridge Journal of Economics* devoted a special issue entirely to new developments in Sraffian studies with contributions from a "who's who" list of prominent Sraffian economists. While the issue is a "must read" for anyone wishing to keep abreast of ongoing research in the field, not a single one of fifteen articles addresses normative issues as such.

This chapter departs from the belief that in the twenty-first century the moral aspect of income distribution should not be sidestepped through methodological artifice, as Marx did, nor avoided, as Sraffians have largely done. There is an urgent need to address the moral aspect of income distribution head on, as do most modern philosophers writing about distributive justice, and as most citizen-activists do as well in a post-occupy environment. But since neither Marxists nor Sraffians have provided a moral critique of capitalism along these lines, we must deduce implicit critiques in each theory, and extrapolate from them before we can compare them.

Marxian Critique

It would only be a slight exaggeration to say that everything Marx ever wrote was a critique of capitalism, and everything he ever did was aimed at helping workers organize to replace capitalism – a system in which they were a subordinate class – with socialism – a system in which they become the new ruling class. Indeed, his unapologetic political advocacy is what prevents some economists from treating him seriously as a contributor to "positive" economics.

Marx wrote about how capitalism turns human beings into a commodity he called "labor power," and thereby "alienates" us from what makes us a unique species; "alienates" us from one another as we lose sight of the relations between people which the trade of commodities implies; and "alienates" us from the products we produce (Marx 1970). Marx wrote about how capitalism deskills and dehumanizes workers. And he argued that exploitation of labor is intrinsic to capitalism since it is the *sine qua non* for positive profits.

But for all of the power and poignancy of Marx's critique, he never provided an explicit argument for why profit income is unfair. And while he subjected various claims by apologists that profits are deserved to ridicule, he never provided serious rebuttal. In his defense, Marx would be the first to stipulate that he doesn't "do" moral critique, and point out that anyone looking for an explicit moral critique of capitalism in his work obviously did not understand his intellectual project. Nonetheless, specifically with regard to distributive justice, Marx's critique of capitalism does not satisfy standards of twenty-first-century moral philosophy.

There are many Marxists who claim this as a virtue. And I will not dispute that here. I will simply observe that I agree with many today who expect a critical evaluation of capitalism to include a straightforward presentation of the case that capitalism systematically distributes income unfairly, including compelling rebuttals to various arguments to the contrary. While Marx himself declined to provide this, as explained in chapter 2, Michio Morishima proved a theorem in 1974 that many Marxists consider to be the definitive word on the immorality of income distribution under capitalism. As already explained, according to Morishima's fundamental Marxian theorem, if and only if the rate of exploitation of labor is positive will the rate of profit be positive. Modern Marxists take it that the implication is perfectly clear for anyone who insists on thinking in moralistic terms: If profits necessarily come from exploiting labor, profits must be unfair, and capitalists' profit income must be unjustified.

Morishima: positive rate of exploitation → positive profit rate

Sraffian Critique

Sraffians have traditionally insisted on sticking to "positive" economics – analysis, explanation, and prediction – and shied away from "normative economics" – evaluating outcomes as desirable or undesirable. But unlike Marx and Marxists, who make abundantly clear that they find capitalism seriously flawed and socialism overwhelmingly superior, Sraffians have largely kept their "political opinions" to themselves. Sraffa himself was a friend and political ally of Antonio Gramsci, leader of the Italian Communist Party – providing Gramsci with books and writing materials when Gramsci was imprisoned by Mussolini from 1926 to 1935. And other prominent Sraffians have openly sympathized with the socialist cause. However, many prominent Sraffians are not anti-capitalist or pro-socialist, and all have gone to great lengths to keep their political views separate from their work as Sraffian economists.

As we have seen, the basic Sraffa model provides a logically consistent and rigorous theoretical explanation of the relationship between wages, profits, and prices in capitalist economies. However, while the theory tells us there are an infinite number of combinations of average wage and profit rates that are possible in any capitalist economy, and therefore that there is a great deal of "wiggle room" for the bargaining power of capitalists and workers to affect where any particular capitalist economy will fall on the wage-profit frontier determined by its technological capabilities $\{\mathbf{A}, \mathbf{L}\}$, as traditionally presented there is no moral dimension to the Sraffa model. In other words, the model does not tell us that some pairs of wage and profit rates are equitable while others are not. In particular, it does not tell us if capitalists are unfairly exploiting workers whenever the rate of profit is above zero.

Since a major goal of Sraffa and many of his followers was to point out inconsistencies, ambiguities, and logical flaws in neoclassical "positive" economics, it was no doubt tempting to initially avoid muddying waters unnecessarily by introducing a "normative" component to their theory. But with the benefit of hindsight it appears to have been a strategic mistake to maintain silence on the obvious moral implications of their analysis. While a few intellectually honest neoclassical theorists have acknowledged that elements of the Sraffian critique are "technically" correct, it has led to no major reworking of mainstream microeconomic theory, and is acknowledged in footnotes in mainstream graduate economic texts with decreasing frequency.

While eschewing normative implications won little recognition from economists in the mainstream of the profession, unfortunately it rendered Sraffian economics unattractive to many political economists who were understandably reluctant to abandon a theory that linked profits to the exploitation of labor for a "bloodless" framework, even if it was devoid of technical flaws. This is most unfortunate because the analysis using the basic Sraffa model not only avoids logical inconsistencies and misleading predictions in the Marxian explanation of price and income determination, the fundamental Sraffian theorem (FST) points toward a more straightforward moral critique of capitalism than the fundamental Marxian theorem (FMT) as well.

As explained in chapter 2, the fundamental Sraffian theorem (FST) says: If and only if there is a physical surplus of goods after wages have been paid will profits be positive. In other words, if and only if those who produce goods are deprived of some of the surplus goods they produce can capitalists have positive profits. Clearly there is an obvious, moral critique of capitalist profits implied by the FST.

FST: profits only happen when there's a surplus

FMT.

Comparing the Marxian and Sraffian Moral Critiques

The issue is not whether one of the "fundamental" theorems is true and the other is false. Both theorems are true – that is, there is no error in their proofs. Moreover, as mentioned in chapter 2, it can be proved that if the FST is true the FMT must also be true, and if the FMT is true then the FST must be true, i.e. FMS ↔ FMT (see theorem 22 in Hahnel 2017). But this does not mean there is nothing to choose between the two theorems. Is the moral critique implied by the FST more or less straightforward and compelling than the critique implied by the FMT?

First of all, notice that the FST uses no concepts which are not familiar to all economists today. Goods are measured in appropriate physical units. The economic surplus is defined in physical units of goods. And prices and the rate of profit are defined exactly as they are in standard economics. In contrast, the FMT analyzes the economy in terms of labor values, and hinges on a ratio defined in terms of labor values. Since the labor theory of value is foreign to all who are not Marxist economists, the FST has a clear advantage regarding ease of communication. If a point could not be made without defining concepts beyond the usual arsenal of concepts, there would be no alternative. But clearly this is not the case since FMS ↔ FMT.

What does the FMT say? The FMT "proves" that profits are only possible if the *rate of exploitation* is positive. But while the word "exploitation" certainly implies that workers have been treated unfairly, what is labeled the "rate of exploitation" in Marxian theory is in fact simply a technical ratio defined in terms of labor values, $(1-\mathbf{Vb})/\mathbf{Vb}$. Absent an explicit argument that when $(1-\mathbf{Vb})/\mathbf{Vb} > 0$ workers are unjustly harmed the moral critique of profits implicit in the FMT rests entirely on Marx's choice of a name, or label, for the ratio $(1-\mathbf{Vb})/\mathbf{Vb}$ – *rate of exploitation*. In effect, we have conviction via semantics. How do Marxists respond if someone asks: Why is it unfair if $(1-\mathbf{Vb})/\mathbf{Vb} > 0$?

What does the FST say? The FST "proves" that profits are only possible if those who produce a surplus of goods are deprived of some of those goods they produced. As in the Marxian formulation, saying something rigorously requires formal precision: In this case, profits are only possible if $\text{dom}[\mathbf{A}+\mathbf{bL}] < 1$. And it is also true that conviction via the FST hinges on the word "deprived." But in this case the word is true to common usage, it is not a pejorative label placed on a technical ratio. If something is taken away from those who produced it, it is consistent with common usage to say they were "deprived" of part of what they produced, and assume we have a clear *prima facie* case of injury, or injustice. Again, someone might ask: Why is it unfair to deprive someone of part of what they produced? And below I will argue that we *do* need to answer this question, rather than simply assume the answer is obvious. We need to consider whether people who did not produce goods may have a legitimate moral claim on them nonetheless. Even so, it seems that the *prima facie* case that profits imply that workers have been unjustly treated is more straightforward and compelling in its Sraffian formulation than in its Marxian formulation.

In sum, the Sraffa model makes clear that it is the economy that is productive, and when capitalists who do no work receive profits, employees who do all the work necessarily receive less than what they produced. There is no need to elaborate a labor value theory of prices to make this point; no need to define a complicated technical ratio defined in terms of labor values, $(1-\textbf{Vb})/\textbf{Vb}$; and no misleading identification of one input to production in particular that holds the key to the origins of profit, when in fact every input could be used to tell the same story. The surplus approach identifies the actual goods and services workers produce which capitalists manage to appropriate. In an era experiencing the most rapid increase in economic inequality in history it seems appropriate to present the case that capitalists are parasites simply and boldly. And if it can be done without resort to introducing concepts like the labor theory of value that are unfamiliar to most economists today, all the better.

However, having done so we should now proceed more cautiously. While Sraffian theory may provide the strongest *prima facie* case that capitalists are parasites living off what others produce, and therefore should be sufficient to bind them over for trial, the accused still have a right to a formal trial where they are represented by competent counsel and presumed innocent until proven guilty. Even if capitalists do none of the work, is it possible that they "contribute" something else that merits reward? Is it possible that they make some "sacrifice" that deserves compensation? Moreover, are we sure we have arrested all those guilty of the crime of economic injustice? Is it possible that not only capitalists but also some workers we have implicitly exonerated by calling them "producers" are also guilty, and belong in the dock along with capitalists?

Rebutting Arguments in Defense of Profits

Capitalists have long had the finest legal defense team money can buy to argue their case. And because it is obvious, and therefore undeniable, their attorneys stipulate that capitalists do no work, but argue that their clients "contribute" to the social endeavor in other ways that merit compensation. The capitalist defense team has argued that their clients merit reward because they "contribute" innovation, because they "contribute" the plant and machinery where their employees work, because they abstain from consumption in order to "contribute" the wage fund workers need while working, and because they take risks and merit compensation for doing so. Failure to offer direct rebuttal to these arguments weakens the moral case against capitalism, and might lead a jury to put aside the *prima facie* case and vote for acquittal.

The Marxist critique sidesteps the main argument in defense of capitalist profits by implicitly defining "contribution" as "contribution to the *value* of goods produced." Since "value" in the Marxian framework is hours of labor done embodied in goods and services, those who do no labor cannot possibly contribute "value." In short, Marxism convicts capitalists of the crime of exploitation on the basis of a clever tautology. However, the critique based on the fundamental Sraffian theorem also assumes away the moral case for capitalist profits through semantics. While more direct and to the point, and therefore arguably more compelling than the Marxist critique, nonetheless by implicitly assuming that the act of working is solely responsible for producing goods, any possibility that non-workers might contribute in other ways, and therefore merit reward, is assumed away by semantics, rather than addressed directly. In the history of economic thought we can find several theories which attempt to justify the moral legitimacy of profits on grounds that capitalists do contribute something of importance which merits reward, even if they do none of the actual work to produce goods and services.

Joseph Schumpeter, for example, defended *profits as reward for innovation.* There is no call to dispute that the major reason a large surplus of goods and services can be produced by workers is precisely because of technological changes which increase labor productivity introduced over many, many years, which have been incorporated into the economic structure to continually increase economic productivity. However, the question is whether capitalists deserve credit for this highly valuable "contribution," and if profits are truly payment for innovations that increase labor productivity.

Here it is important to distinguish between different roles, since sometimes the same person plays more than one role in the economy. "Inventor" is our name for the "creators" of technological change, and "royalty" is the customary name for payments to inventors. Capitalists, on the other hand, are owners of firms, and "profit" is the name for payments to capitalists. If a capitalist happens to *also* be an inventor, then the same person will receive both kinds of income. But that does not mean that profits are a payment for invention. On the other hand, if the inventor is an employee of a capitalist the inventor will be paid a salary, and perhaps a bonus by her capitalist employer who presumably still receives profits. If there is no patent the capitalist will receive temporary super profits from using the invention of his employee, but these super profits will be competed away as the innovation is copied by other capitalists. If there is a patent the capitalist will receive super profits for longer, and/or royalties if he licenses others to use the invention of his employee, which, as her employer, he owns.

However, super profits and royalties are clearly different from the normal, or uniform, rate of profit capitalists receive. To demonstrate, suppose there are no new inventions and therefore $\rho(l) = 0$. Would capitalist profits be zero? The simple Sraffa model makes clear that even if there are no innovations, as long as the economy was productive after wages are paid the rate of profit will be positive. So the profits we are in search of a justification for have nothing to do with payments for the creative labor that yields productive new innovations.

The argument that all *"factors of production," including "capital," deserve payment according to the value of their marginal revenue product* is often associated with J. B. Clark. There are two problems with this argument which other economists have pointed out. Joan Robinson pointed out the first problem when she observed that however "productive" a machine may be, its productivity hardly constitutes a moral argument for paying anything to its owner. Robinson's point can be applied to any argument in any production function. Just because adding another unit of some input will increase the value of output by some amount does not mean that the owner of the input, even should the owner be the worker herself, *deserves* a payment of precisely that magnitude – neither more nor less.

Sraffa and his followers raise a second problem. Sraffians argue convincingly that any attempt to define and measure a marginal product for something called "capital," as distinct from the marginal products of particular heterogeneous capital goods, is doomed to failure. The problem, as well as the explanation for why it is irresolvable, was succinctly stated by Kurz and Salvadori:

> The notion of a production function requires that a single level of output be associated with any given amount of productive resources employed. However, with capital goods represented by their value in

the production function, with different levels of the rate of profit the value of the same set of capital goods would generally also be different. This however runs counter to the uniqueness of the relation between output and the amount of productive resources used as inputs. The criticism reported is derived from the fact that relative prices, and thus also the prices of capital goods, generally depend on income distribution.

(Kurz and Salvadori 1995: 445)

This argument applies to production functions for particular goods as well as an aggregate production function, which was the initial subject of debate in the Cambridge capital controversy. Only in models where there is a single produced good, which serves both as the sole consumption good and the sole "capital good," does this problem not arise.

The argument that *profits are a justifiable reward for "abstinence," or "waiting"* on the part of capitalists is commonly attributed to Nassau Senior. However, it can be found in the work of Jevons, Bohm–Bawerk, Walras, Wicksell, and Marshall as well. In essence the argument is this: (1) If workers have no income, wages must be advanced from a "wage fund" for them to be able to work and produce anything at all. And when workers are equipped with more means of production they are more productive than when they have less. (2) If nobody saved – i.e. if nobody "abstained" from consuming all their income – there would be no "wage fund" and no investment goods produced, and productivity would cease (absent a wage fund) or decline (as capital goods depreciate). (3) Ergo, by saving and investing part of their income capitalists make possible production of a larger surplus than would otherwise occur, and therein lies their valuable "contribution" deserving reward.

What would happen if nobody saved any of their income during a year? In this case all production would take the form of consumption goods and no investment goods would be produced at all, leaving workers only that part of capital stocks which did not depreciate to work with the following year. Clearly their productivity would suffer, and we might well conclude that anyone who saves – so investment goods can be produced along with consumption goods – is a hero deserving some appropriate reward. But then the conclusion should be that *anyone* who saves out of their income deserves some appropriate reward, not that profit income is deserved because capitalists save part of it.

Suppose we were trying to explain why a worker deserves her wages. Would we do so by arguing that because she saves part of her wages her wages are deserved? In which case, would we then concede that if she fails to save, her wages are undeserved? Would we conclude that only the part of her wages she saves are deserved, while the part of her wages she consumes are undeserved? In case it is not obvious that income is not justified on the basis of what one subsequently may choose to do with it, consider a group of pirates who out and out plunder from others this year, but then save part of their plunder. Would we say these pirates deserve their plunder because they save part of it, and thereby allow the economy to produce investment goods along with consumption goods?[1] Just as pirate booty cannot be justified by what pirates may choose to do with it, capitalist profits cannot be justified because they save part it. The fact that capitalists abstain from consuming all of their profit income has nothing to do with whether or not that profit income was deserved in the first place.[2]

Finally, it is sometimes argued that profits are a residual, which means that unlike others whose incomes are presumably contractually guaranteed, *capitalists bear risk, and not only require, but deserve compensation for doing so.* In the real world there is uncertainty, and therefore risk. In the real world some businesses, and perhaps some industries, are riskier than others – giving rise to a spectrum of profit rates. Differences in profit rates among capitalists due to differences in the risks they incur are not only predictable, but we can even stipulate that they are morally justifiable on grounds that an expected value of $100 with a variance of $50 is not as valuable to most humans as a 100% probability of $100. And if profit income is less certain than wage income on average, then an average rate of profit *somewhat* greater than zero can be justified on similar grounds. But this does not provide either an explanation or a moral justification for an average expected rate of profit that is not only positive but in excess of what is required to compensate for its greater uncertainty than other forms of income.

The Sraffa framework can help us distinguish between profits which are due to the fact that profit income is less certain than wage income, and profits that have nothing to do with risk. Unlike the real world, in a Sraffian framework there is no uncertainty, and therefore there is no risk! In a Sraffian framework if the rate of profit exceeds zero it cannot be because capitalists are incurring risk. In a Sraffian framework as soon as $dom(\mathbf{A}+\mathbf{bL}) < 1$ capitalists will receive an $r > 0$ with as much certainty as the $w > 0$ workers receive. And it is *that* $r > 0$ which requires a justification. In sum, what the Sraffian framework makes clear – in this case because of its very simplicity in abstracting from uncertainty – is that there are profits in real capitalist economies which have nothing to do with risk, and therefore cannot be either explained or justified as reward for risk.[3]

In sum, there is no need to deny that risk deserves some reward. There is no need to deny that if workers had no income to live on while working they would produce very little indeed, absent a fund to pay wages in advance. There is no need to deny that if workers had no capital goods to work with they would produce only a paltry amount. What is asserted is that once the economy is sufficiently productive and wages remain sufficiently low, there will be profits in excess of what can be either explained or justified as reward for risk. What is disputed is that capitalists deserve to have the funds they use to advance workers their wages and equip workers with machines to work with in exchange for profits.[4] In sum, what is disputed is the claim that there is something meritorious in the behavior of capitalists that justifies the great bulk of their profits. Moreover, nothing capitalists choose to do with their profits can retroactively provide a justification for why they received them in the first place.

Of course if someone owns the wage funds, machines, and technologies – if they are someone's legal property, to use and contract over their use as they please – their owners will often be able to secure a payment from others who lack some form of wherewithal without which they cannot work productively. But in this case the compensation capitalists receive is *tribute* they are in a position to *extract* from those who work, and as explained below, the size of the tribute they will be able to extract will largely be determined by how much less fiercely they must compete among them- selves for employees than workers must compete among themselves for employment – none of which has anything to do with "just deserts."

What Counts: Contribution or Sacrifice?

At this point it is useful to ask what a philosopher might say about our evidentiary hearing and how the formal trial has proceeded so far. Because philosophers would be likely to ask what theory of distributive justice was the basis for the trial, and therefore what testimony was relevant or irrelevant, and what criteria the judge was going to instruct the jury to consider when deliberating over guilt and innocence. Philosophers would no doubt point out that so far both the prosecution and defense have implicitly assumed that the relevant criterion is contribution – who contributes to production and who does not, and how much anyone contributes. Philosophers – notorious sticklers for questioning first principles – would point out that there is another possibility: Namely, that the amount of goods and services one *deserves* depends on what *sacrifices* one makes in producing goods and services, not on how much one *contributes* to the value of goods and services produced. Considering arguments for and against three different simple maxims is a useful starting point once the issue of relevant criteria has been raised.

Maxim 1: *Payment according to the value of the contribution of one's labor and the contribution of the productive property one owns*

The rationale behind maxim 1 is that people should get out of an economy what they and their productive possessions contribute to the economy. If we think of the goods and services, or benefits of an economy, as a giant pot of stew, the idea is that individuals contribute to how big and rich the stew will be by their labor and by the productive assets they bring to the kitchen. If my labor and productive assets make the stew bigger or richer than your labor and assets, then according to maxim 1 it is only fair that I eat more stew, or richer morsels, than you do.

While this rationale has obvious appeal, it has a major problem we might call the *Rockefeller grandson problem*. According to maxim 1 the grandson of a Rockefeller with a large inheritance of productive property *should* eat 1000 times as much stew as a highly trained, highly productive, hardworking son of a pauper — even if Rockefeller's grandson doesn't work a day in his life while the pauper's son works for fifty years producing goods or providing services of great benefit to others. This will inevitably occur if we count the contribution of productive property people own, and if people own different amounts of machinery, or what is the same thing, different amounts of stock in corporations that own the machinery, since bringing a cooking pot, or better yet a stove, to the economy "kitchen" increases the size and quality of the stew we can make just as surely as peeling potatoes and stirring the pot does. So anyone who considers it *unfair* when the idle grandson of a Rockefeller consumes more than a hardworking, productive son of a pauper cannot accept maxim 1 as their theory of distributive justice. But what if those with more productive property acquired it through some greater *merit*? Would not the income they accrue from this property then be justifiable? If some people acquire more productive property than others through inheritance, luck, force, or fraud it is relatively easy to explain why the extra income they receive as a result is unfair (see Hahnel 2005). But what if people come to have more productive property because they use income they earned fairly to purchase more productive property than others?

There is a moral problem regarding income from productive property even if the productive property was purchased with income we stipulate was fairly earned in the first place. Labor and credit markets allow people with productive wealth to capture part of the increase in productivity of *other people* that results when others work with the productive wealth. Moreover, the share captured by wealthy employers as profits, and wealthy lenders as interest, is determined by forces in labor and credit markets with no claim to yielding fair shares: It is determined by the laws of supply and demand and bargaining power. So whether or not and to what extent the profit or interest owners of productive wealth receive is merited must be carefully examined.

Even if we stipulate that some compensation is justified by a meritorious action that occurred *once* in the past, there is a problem: Labor and credit markets allow those who own more productive property to parlay it into *permanently* higher incomes which *increase* over time with no further meritorious behavior on their part.[5] This creates the dilemma that ownership of productive property *even if purchased with income that was justly acquired, and even if deserving of **some** compensation*, generally gives rise to additional income that becomes unfair at some point, and increasingly so, as time proceeds.[6]

In sum, if unequal accumulations of productive property were the result only of meritorious actions, and if compensation in the form of profits and interest ceased when the social debt was fully repaid, calling property income unfair would seem harsh and unwarranted. On the other hand, if those who own more productive property acquired it through inheritance, luck, or unfair advantage, or because once they have more productive property than others they can accumulate ever more with no further meritorious behavior by participating as employers in labor markets or lenders in credit markets, then calling the unequal outcomes that result from differences in wealth unfair seems perfectly appropriate. We discuss what studies of empirical evidence reveal about what part of wealth today is derived from these different sources below.

Maxim 2: Payment according to the value of one's personal contribution only

When substitution between legitimate arguments in production functions is assumed, marginal physical products for inputs can be calculated. The valid

Sraffian case against the positive neoclassical theory that when markets are competitive what neoclassicals call "factors of production" *will* receive payments equal to their marginal revenue products is based on two arguments: (1) While a particular machine may be a proper argument in a production function, and therefore have a positive marginal revenue product, "capital in general" is not a proper argument in production functions, and therefore the marginal revenue product of "capital" cannot be deduced from production functions, much less be equated with the rate of profit. (2) Because there is an economic "surplus," income distribution cannot be deduced solely from marginal revenue products of inputs which are proper arguments in production functions.

To illustrate: If we assume that competition among capitalists is so fierce that it compels capitalists to continue hiring inputs as long as the rate of profit from doing so remains positive, we get the standard neoclassical conclusions: (a) the rate of profit will be driven down to zero, (b) all inputs, including every category of labor, will be hired up to the point where its marginal revenue product is equal to its price, and therefore (c) every input will be paid its marginal revenue product. But notice that these conclusions derive from the assumption that competition among capitalists is so fierce that they compete away any share of the economic surplus, no matter how large that surplus may be. If instead we assume that competition among capitalists is somewhat less fierce so they do not entirely compete away any share in the economic surplus, i.e. competition only compels capitalists to accept some rate of profit, r, greater than zero, the conclusions become rather different: (a') the rate of profit will only be driven down to some rate greater than zero, (b') in which case all inputs, including every category of labor, will be hired up to the point where its marginal revenue product is equal to its price *times* $(1+r)$, and therefore (c') every input will be paid $r/(1+r)$MRP *less* than its marginal revenue product.[7]

In other words, the positive neoclassical marginal revenue product theory of payments to inputs in production does not address, much less solve, the question of what the "normal" or "long-run" rate of profit will be. What rate of profit capitalists will be compelled to accept, and why, is not answered by the marginal productivity theory of what different physical inputs in production will be paid. The answer to that question hinges on how fierce the competition *among* capitalists for employees is, and therefore how large or small their collective share of the economic surplus will be; compared to how fierce the competition *among* workers for employment is, and therefore how large or small their collective share of the economic surplus will be. Differences in marginal productivities *among* workers will affect how labor's share of the economic surplus is distributed among workers, But it is the *relative* fierceness of competition among workers and among capitalists that will determine the share of the economic surplus each group captures, and the marginal productivities of legitimate arguments in production functions tell us nothing about this whatsoever.

What the Sraffa model brings to this discussion is the helpful reminder that irrespective of whatever all inputs' marginal productivities may be, as long as $dom[A+bL] < 1$ the rate of profit will be positive. In other words, the question of how high r will be for any given technology, $\{A,L\}$, reduces to the question of how high b, the hourly real wage bundle, will be. To summarize, and with the proviso that we are speaking in broad generalities: The *relative* fierceness of competition *among* capitalists and *among* workers will decide how the economic surplus is divided *between* capitalists and workers, while differences in marginal productivities of different categories of labor affect how labor's share of the surplus is divided among workers.

Before proceeding to evaluate maxim 2 it is worth clearing up one last common confusion. What maxim 2 proposes is fair is payment according to the *value* of the contribution of one's labor. While it is common to equate the "value" of the contribution of labor to the marginal revenue product of labor, it is not necessarily the case that the *social value* of the increase in output from another hour of someone's labor is the same as their marginal revenue product. Marginal revenue product, MRP, is equal to marginal physical product, MPP, times price, P. And while MRP is therefore the increase in an employer's revenues from hiring another hour of someone's labor, it is not the same as the increase in social value if the market where the output is sold is non-competitive, or if there are externalities associated with producing or consuming the good.

Whenever there are externalities or goods markets are non-competitive market price systematically misestimates the benefit to society of producing another unit of a good. If the market for a good is less than perfectly competitive its price will exceed its marginal social benefit, and consequently the MRP of all inputs used to make it will exceed their marginal social product, MSP. Similarly, if there are negative external effects associated with producing or consuming a good its market price will exceed its marginal social benefit, and the MRP of inputs used will exceed their MSP. While if there are positive external effects marginal revenue products will fall short of marginal social benefits, and the MRP of inputs used will be less than their MSP.

In sum, there are multiple reasons that labor will not be paid an amount equal to its marginal social product in capitalist economies: All workers will be paid [r/(1+r)]MRP less than their MRP. The MRPs of workers in non-competitive industries and industries with negative externalities will exceed their MSPs. While the MSPs of workers in any industries with positive externalities will exceed their MRPs. But the issue here is whether payments equal to marginal social products are fair, not whether capitalist economies will pay people according to their marginal social products – which they will *not* for all the reasons just explained.

Having clarified all this, we are finally ready to consider maxim 2: As long as substitution between different legitimate inputs in production is possible, we can in theory measure their marginal social products, including the marginal social products of different categories of labor. Are payments equal to the marginal social product of one's labor fair and just? While those who support maxim 2 find property income unjustifiable, advocates for maxim 2 hold that everyone has a moral right to the "fruits of their own labor," i.e. payment equal to the marginal social product of one's labor. The rationale for this has a powerful appeal: If my labor contributes more to social wellbeing, i.e. my marginal social product is higher, it is only fair that I receive more. Not only am I not exploiting others, they would be exploiting me by paying me less than the social value of my personal contribution.

First of all, the marginal product, or contribution of an input to production, depends as much on the number of units of that input used, and on the quantity and quality of other, complementary inputs, as on any intrinsic quality of the input itself – which immediately undermines the moral imperative behind maxim 2. But besides the fact that the marginal products of different kinds of labor depend very much on the number of people in each labor category in the first place, and on the quantity and quality of non-labor inputs available to them, most differences in people's personal productivities are due to intrinsic qualities of people themselves over which people have little control. No amount of eating and weight lifting will give an average individual a 6 foot 9 inch frame with 380 pounds of muscle. Yet professional football players in the United States receive hundreds of times more than an average salary because those attributes make the value of their contribution outrageously high in the context of US sports culture. Just as Joan Robinson argued that however "productive" a machine or piece of land may be, that hardly constitutes a moral argument for paying anything to its owner; one can argue that however "productive" a 380-pound physique or a high IQ may be, that doesn't mean the owner of this trait deserves more income than someone less gifted who works as hard and sacrifices as much. The bottom line is that the "genetic lottery" influences how valuable one's personal contribution will be. Yet the genetic lottery is no more fair than the inheritance lottery, which implies that as a conception of economic justice maxim 2 suffers from the same fatal flaw as maxim 1.

In defense of maxim 2 it is frequently argued that while talent may not deserve reward, to make talent productive requires training, and those who undergo extra training deserve extra reward. In this vein it is frequently argued that doctors' high salaries are justifiable compensation for all their extra years of education. First of all, it is important not to confuse the cost of someone's training to society – which consists mostly of the *trainer's* time and energy, and scarce social resources like books, computers, microscopes, libraries, and classrooms – with costs borne by the *trainee*. If teachers and educational facilities are paid for at public expense – that is, if we have a universal public education system – and if students are paid a living stipend – so they forgo no income while in school – then the only cost borne by the student consists of their discomfort from time spent in school. But even the personal suffering we endure as students must be properly compared. While many educational programs are less personally enjoyable than time spent in leisure, comparing discomfort during school with comfort during leisure is usually not the relevant comparison. The relevant comparison is with the discomfort of others in the same age cohort experience who are working instead of going to school. So to the extent that education is paid for publicly rather than privately, students receive a living stipend, and the personal discomfort of schooling is no greater than the discomfort others incur while working, the claim that those with higher social marginal products due to greater education deserve higher reward because they underwent extra training does not hold up under scrutiny.

In sum, we might call the problem with maxim 2 the *doctor–garbage collector problem*. If education were free all the way through medical school, how could it be fair to pay a brain surgeon who is on the first tee at his country club by 2pm even on the four days a week he works, ten times more than a garbage collector who works under miserable conditions forty plus hours a week? Which brings us to a third distributive maxim.

Maxim 3: Payment according to effort, or the personal sacrifices one makes in work

Whereas differences in personal contribution will be due to differences in talent, training, job assignment, luck, and effort, the only factor that deserves extra compensation according to maxim 3 is extra effort. By "effort" is meant personal sacrifice in work for the sake of the social good. Of course effort can take many forms. It may be working more hours. It may be performing less pleasant tasks. It may be working in more dangerous or unhealthy work environments. Or it may be working at greater intensity, i.e. what is commonly called exerting more "effort." It may also consist of undergoing training that is less gratifying than the training experiences of others, or less pleasant than time others spend working who train less. The underlying rationale for maxim 3 is that people should eat from the stew pot according to the sacrifices they made to cook the stew. According to maxim 3 no other consideration, beside differential sacrifice, can justify one person eating more stew than another.

One argument for why sacrifice deserves reward is that people have control over how much they sacrifice. I can decide to work longer hours, or work harder, whereas I cannot decide to be 6 foot 9 or have a high IQ. It is commonly considered unjust to punish someone for something she could do nothing about. On those grounds paying someone less just because she is not strong or smart violates a fundamental precept of fair play. On the other hand, if someone doesn't work as long or hard as the rest of us, we don't feel it is inappropriate to punish her by paying her less because she *could* have worked longer or harder if she had chosen to. In the case of reward according to effort, avoiding punishment is possible, whereas in the case of reward according to contribution it often is not.

Nor is there any reason for society to frown on those who prefer to make fewer sacrifices as long as they are willing to accept less economic benefits to go along with their lesser sacrifice. There is no reason that just because people enter into a system of equitable cooperation with others this precludes leaving the sacrifice/benefit trade-off to personal choice. Maxim 3 simply balances any differences in the burdens people choose to bear with commensurate differences in the benefits they receive. This is perhaps the strongest argument for reward according to sacrifice. Even if all were not equally *able* to make sacrifices, extra benefits to compensate for extra burdens seems fair. When people enter into economic cooperation with one another, for the arrangement to be just should not all participants benefit equally? Since each participant bears burdens as well as enjoys benefits, it is equalization of *net* benefits, benefits enjoyed minus burdens borne, that makes the economic cooperation fair. So if some bear more of the burdens justice requires that they be compensated with benefits commensurate with their greater sacrifice. Only then will all enjoy equal *net* benefits. Only then will the system of economic cooperation be treating all participants equally, i.e. giving equal weight or priority to the interests of all participants. Notice that even if some are more able to sacrifice than others, i.e. even if "sacrifice" is to some extent "conditioned" and not entirely "freely chosen," the outcome for both the more and less able to sacrifice is the same when extra sacrifices are rewarded. In this way all receive the same net benefits from economic cooperation irrespective of any differences in their abilities to contribute *or* to make sacrifices.

Many who object to maxim 3 as a distributive principle raise questions about measuring sacrifice, or about conflicts between reward according to sacrifice and economic efficiency. But measurement problems, or conflicts between equity and efficiency are *not* objections to maxim 3 as an appropriate conception of what is fair, i.e. they are not objections *on equity grounds*. To reject maxim 3 because effort or sacrifice may be difficult to measure or because rewarding sacrifice may reduce efficiency is not to reject it because it is unfair. No matter how weighty these arguments may prove to be, they are not arguments against maxim 3 on grounds that it somehow fails to accurately express what it means for the distribution of burdens and benefits in a system of economic cooperation to be just, or fair. Moreover, even should it prove that distributive justice is difficult to achieve because it is difficult to measure effort accurately, or costly to achieve because to do so generates inefficiency, one presumably would still wish to know exactly what this elusive or costly distributive justice *is*.

Even for those who reject contribution based theories of distributive justice like maxim 1 and 2 as inherently flawed because people's abilities to contribute are often different through no fault of their own – as do all modern egalitarian philosophers – there is still a problem with maxim 3 from a moral point of view that we might call the *AIDS victim problem*. Suppose someone has made average sacrifices for fifteen years, and accordingly consumed an average amount. Suddenly they contract AIDS through no fault of their own. In the early 1990s a medical treatment program for an AIDS victim often cost close to a million dollars. That is, the cost to society of providing humane care for an AIDS victim was roughly a million dollars. If we limit people's consumption to the level warranted by their efforts, we would have to deny AIDS victims humane treatment, which is hard to defend on moral grounds. Of course this is where another maxim comes to mind: *payment according to need*. Whether taking differences of need into consideration is required by distributive justice, or is required instead for an economy to be *humane* is debatable. However, at the risk of scandalizing professional philosophers, as long as we conclude that ignoring either differences in sacrifice or differences in need is morally unacceptable, can't we conclude that the issue has been reduced to a question of semantics?

Conclusion: Guilty as Charged!

The fundamental Sraffian theorem arguably provides a more straightforward and compelling *prima facie* case that capitalists are parasites than does the fundamental Marxian theorem. However, that charge, like the implicit critique of capitalist profits in Marxian theory, was also based on a contribution-based theory of distributive justice. In both theories the presumption is that how much people are entitled to should be determined by how much they produce. In the Marxian formulation workers are wronged because capitalists deny them the full "value" of what they produce each hour, i.e. because $\mathbf{Vb} < 1$, while in the Sraffian formulation workers are wronged because capitalists deny them all the actual goods and services they produce each hour, i.e. because $\mathrm{dom}(\mathbf{A+bL}) < 1$. In both formulations capitalists get more than they deserve if they get anything at all, because they produce nothing – neither "value" in the Marxian formulation, nor actual goods and services in the Sraffian formulation. However, if the critique of contribution-based theories presented above is valid, does not this imply that a jury might acquit capitalists upon reconsideration?

After considering all of the arguments for and against the three maxims suppose the judge presiding over our trial ruled in favor of maxim 3. In other words, suppose the judge ruled that in her courtroom contribution was not the relevant consideration. Suppose she ruled that henceforth only evidence regarding reward compared to sacrifice was relevant testimony. And suppose she instructed the jury to consider only sacrifice and ignore contribution when judging whether or not anyone was guilty of being a parasite. What would our trial look like?

Now the prosecuting attorney must argue that capitalists receive profits greater than their sacrifices, while workers on the whole receive wages less than their sacrifices warrant. It no longer matters who contributes more or less. It does not matter what form anyone's contribution takes. What matters is only who gets more than they sacrifice, and who gets less than they sacrifice. What matters is only if compensation is commensurate with sacrifice, exceeds sacrifice, or falls short of sacrifice.

In our mock trial if the defense team for capitalists wants to argue that capitalists deserve profits they must explain concretely what sacrifice capitalists have made. If the rate of profit is positive and they cannot produce credible evidence of any sacrifice, their client will be found guilty, as charged. And even if the capitalist defense team produces evidence of some sacrifice on the part of their client, they must demonstrate that their client's profits, which accrue at a compound rate *indefinitely*, do not exceed the magnitude of whatever sacrifice capitalists made *once only* by "abstaining" from consuming part of what is usually a considerable income in an initial year.

Most economists who have studied the causes of unequal wealth believe that differences in ownership of productive property which accumulate within a single generation due to the behavior of individuals themselves are small compared to the differences in wealth that develop due to inheritance, luck, unfair advantage, and accumulation that is without merit. Lester Thurow (1996) estimated that between 50 and 70% of all wealth in the US is inherited. Daphne Greenwood and Edward Wolff (1992) estimated that 50 to 70% of the wealth of households under age fifty was inherited. Laurence Kotlikoff and Lawrence Summers (1981) estimated that as much as 80% of personal wealth came either from direct inheritance or the income on inherited wealth. A study published by United for a Fair Economy in 1997 titled "Born on Third Base" found that of the 400 on the 1997 Forbes list of wealthiest individuals and families in the US, 42% inherited their way onto the list; another 6% inherited wealth in excess of $50 million, and another 7% started life with at least $1 million.

These are examples of the kind of testimony that the prosecution would now bring to our trial of capitalists and rentiers as parasites. Surely the prosecutor would introduce all 685 pages of Thomas Piketty's *Capital in the Twenty-First Century* in evidence as well. But I can think of no better choice to give the prosecution's final argument than Edward Bellamy, who put it this way over a hundred years ago:

> You may set it down as a rule that the rich, the possessors of great wealth, had no moral right to it as based upon desert, for either their fortunes belonged to the class of inherited wealth, or else, when accumulated in a lifetime, necessarily represented chiefly the product of others, more or less forcibly or fraudulently obtained.
>
> *(Bellamy 1970: 113)*

At the end of such a trial the jury might not find all capitalists guilty. However, it is difficult to imagine that a jury selected at random would not find most capitalists guilty on this basis. Moreover, a sound basis for a trial of workers, some of whom might also be guilty of consuming more than their efforts or sacrifices warrant, would have been established.

Notes

1 Note that whether or not we think the pirates deserve some reward for abstaining from consuming part of their plunder, even though it is stipulated that the entire plunder was holy *un*deserved in the first place, is a *different* question.
2 Joan Robinson dismissed this argument with a clever quip in a lecture titled "The Theory of Value Reconsidered" delivered at University College, London in November 1968: "Income from property is not the reward of waiting, it is the reward of employing a good stockbroker."
3 Another way to make this point would be to present the argument in terms of expected values as follows: Stipulate that a profit rate of 10% with probability 0.500 is *not* equivalent to a profit rate of 5% with probability 1.00, but instead is only equivalent to a profit rate of 4% with probability 1.00. In which case it is this "certainty equivalent" profit rate of 4% that the Sraffian framework demonstrates will exist in any economy that is sufficiently productive, and whose real wage is sufficiently low, that requires justification – and cannot be justified as reward for risk. For those concerned about the difference between knowable and unknowable uncertainty, and therefore the difference between insurable and uninsurable risk, the Sraffa framework offers an environment in which *neither* kind of uncertainty exists, and yet positive profits logically emerge if labor productivity is sufficiently high and wages are sufficiently low.
4 Put differently, what is asserted is that workers only lack a wage fund and machines to work with because capitalists deprived them of part of what they produced in the past.
5 Thomas Piketty's exhaustive review of data on inequality of income, capital, and wealth in many countries over long periods of time in Piketty (2014) drives this point home quite clearly.
6 For a simple model that illustrates these important issues see Hahnel (2006).
7 For $r > 0$ employers will stop hiring more of an input when its MRP reaches $(1+r)$ times its price, which implies that inputs will receive $[r/(1+r)]$MRP *less* than their marginal revenue product. So, for example, even if labor markets are competitive, if the rate of profit in the economy is 10% a worker whose MRP is $10 per hour will only be paid $10 − [.10/1.10]$10 = $9.09 per hour, and a worker whose MRP is $20 per hour will only be paid $20 − [.10/1.10]$20 = $18.18 per hour. Clearly differences in worker productivities still lead to differences in wage rates among workers, but as long as $r > 0$ *all* workers will be paid less than their MRPs in a capitalist economy. However, regardless of how inputs *will* be paid in a capitalist economy, the question addressed in this section is whether or not inputs to production, including labor, *should* be paid an amount equal to their MRP, i.e. whether or not MRP payments to the owners of inputs to production are fair and just.

CONCLUSION

In 2017 we have a better formal framework for analyzing the salient properties of capitalism than the labor theory of value available to Marx in the nineteenth century. It's time to make use of it!

- Sraffian theory provides a more straightforward and rigorous explanation of price determination in capitalism than does formal Marxian theory using the labor theory of value.
- Sraffian theory explains why profits are the result of depriving those who produce them of some of the goods they produce, without mis-identifying one of many inputs capitalists purchase as the sole source of their profits.
- Sraffian theory does not mislead us about the effect of technological change on the rate of profit, and helps us understand why Adam Smith's second invisible hand is as unreliable as his first: Just as competitive markets cannot be trusted to allocate scarce productive resources efficiently at any point in time when there are externalities, capitalists cannot be trusted to adopt and reject new technologies to raise labor productivity when the rate of profit is positive. In short, unlike Marxian theory, Sraffian theory demonstrates that perhaps the strongest argument in defense of capitalism – that whatever other flaws it may have, capitalism can be relied on to promote dynamic efficiency – turns out to be untrue.

- Sraffian theory demonstrates that Marx's hypothesis that capital deepening would eventually reduce the rate of profit and lead to a system-ending crisis was a lengthy red herring. Moreover, Sraffian theory is allied with post-Keynesian, neo-Kaleckian, Minskian, and structuralist heterodox macroeconomic schools of thought which provide more rigorous models of crises which are real possibilities, without deceiving us that some "internal contradiction" will inevitably bring capitalism to an end.
- Sraffian theory easily incorporates rents for natural resources into our explanation of price and income determination, and helps us rigorously measure what ecological economists call "environmental throughput" so we can formulate sufficient conditions for environmental sustainability, which do not mislead us into thinking that environmental protection is incompatible with further increases in material living standards.
- Moreover, Sraffian theory does all this using concepts and methodologies that are familiar to economists and the lay public, rather than requiring people to learn a nineteenth-century framework and methodology foreign to all today except Marxists. And as this book demonstrates, Sraffian theory can be presented in a readily accessible way that only requires one to be comfortable with solving two equations in two unknowns.

So why would anyone today persist in any longer using Marxian formal economic theory grounded in the labor theory of value, rather than Sraffian theory instead?

- Marx was, is, and will remain a giant intellectual figure in human history. Like Darwin and Freud, Marx changed our understanding of ourselves forever. Moreover, Marx wrote as much, on as many different subjects as Sraffa wrote little, on a narrow range of topics. So if posed as: Choose Marx or Sraffa – choose a major or a minor intellectual figure – the choice is a no brainer!
- Suppose you are only beginning to suspect that capitalism is not the be-all-and-end-all of economic systems that mainstream economists, mainstream politicians, and the mainstream media would have us believe. Or suppose you have already seen enough damage to feel sure that the capitalist system plays a major role in causing many of our most trenchant problems, and that humanity must surely be capable of organizing our economic affairs in a better way. Why would you reject

the greatest critic of capitalism for an economist few have heard of, whose followers shy away from drawing normative conclusions and refuse to cast judgement on capitalism?

But these are false choices. One need not reject Marx in his entirety, nor look to Sraffa for answers to all questions. Precisely because great intellectual figures address many, large issues, it is predictable that they will make mistakes – mistakes that smaller intellectual figures can subsequently correct. And if we make use of new intellectual tools which become available we can sometimes improve upon earlier theories and arguments. What this book proposes is simply that we substitute superior Sraffian treatments of particular subjects in economics for their formal Marxian counterparts which have become outmoded.

However, I am under no illusions that those in search of a useful radical political economy for the twenty-first century will be inclined to do so unless Sraffians explicitly address the moral illegitimacy of the overwhelming majority of income inequality under capitalism, and afford environmental sustainability the attention it clearly demands. A second goal of this book was to show how Sraffian theory can be extended to do both.

The argument is simple: Radical political economy should honor Great Grandfather Marx for the unpayable debt we owe him. But it is past time we should also take advantage of formal modeling improvements pioneered by Uncle Sraffa – all as we continue to show how Sraffian economics can help us address the two great challenges that face us as the twenty-first century unfolds: Climate change and environmental destruction, and the moral outrage of escalating economic inequality.

REFERENCES

Aglietta, M. 2016. *A Theory of Capitalist Regulation: The US Experience*, reprint edition. London UK: Verso. Original English edition 1979.

Albert, M., L. Cagan, N. Chomsky, R. Hahnel, M. King, L. Sargent, and H. Sklar. 1986. *Liberating Theory*. Boston MA: South End Press.

Alperovitz, G. and L. Daly. 2008. *Unjust Deserts: How the Rich Are Taking Our Common Inheritance*. New York NY: The New Press.

Baran, P. and P. Sweezy. 1966. *Monopoly Capital: An Essay on the American Economic and Social Order*. New York NY: Monthly Review.

Bellamy, E. 1960. *Looking Backward*. New York NY: Signet Classics, the New American Library.

Bellamy, E. 1970. *Equality*, originally published in 1897. Norwalk CT: AMS Press.

Boddy, R. and J. Crotty. 1974. "Class Conflict, Keynesian Policies, and the Business Cycle." *Monthly Review* 26, 5: 1–17.

Bohm-Bawerk, E. 1949. *Karl Marx and the Close of his System*, originally published in German in 1896. New York NY: August M. Kelly. This edition also contains Rudolf Hilferding's response, "Bohm-Bawerk's Criticism of Marx," Ladislav von Bortkiewicz's "On Marx's Fundamental Theoretical Construction in the Third Volume of Capital," and an introduction by Paul Sweezy. Available at: https://mises.org/system/tdf/Karl%20Marx%20and%20the%20Close%20of%20His%20System.pdf?file=1&type=document.

Bowles, S., D. Gordon, and T. Weisskopf. 1983. *Beyond the Wasteland: A Democratic Alternative to Economic Decline*. New York NY: Anchor Press/Doubleday.

Bowles, S., D. Gordon, and T. Weisskopf. 1986. "Power and Profits: The Social Structure of Accumulation and the Profitability of the Postwar US Economy." *Review of Radical Political Economics* 18, 1–2: 132–167.

Bowles, S., D. Gordon, and T. Weisskopf. 1989. "Business Ascendancy and Economic Impasse: A Structural Retrospective on Conservative Economics, 1979–87." *Journal of Economic Perspectives* 3, 1: 107–134.

Burkett, P. 2006. *Marxism and Ecological Economics: Toward a Red and Green Political Economy.* London UK: Palgrave MacMillan.

Dumenil, G. 1980. *De la Valeur aux Prix de Production.* Paris: Economica.

Dumenil, G. 1984. "Beyond the Transformation Riddle: A Labor Theory of Value," *Science and Society* 47, 4: 427–450.

Fine, B. and L. Harris. 1979. *Reading Capital.* New York NY: Columbia University Press.

Foley, D. 1982. "The Value of Money, the Value of Labor Power, and the Marxian Transformation Problem." *Review of Radical Political Economics* 14, 2: 37–47.

Foley, D. 1986. *Understanding Capital: Marx's Economic Theory.* Cambridge MA: Harvard University Press.

Foley, D. 2000. "Recent Developments in the Labor Theory of Value." *Review of Radical Political Economics* 32, 1: 1–39.

Foster, J. B. 1994. *The Vulnerable Planet: A Short Economic History of the Environment.* New York NY: Cornerstone Books.

Foster, J. B. 2000. *Marx's Ecology: Materialism and Nature.* New York NY: Monthly Review.

Foster, J. B. 2002. *Ecology Against Capitalism.* New York NY: Monthly Review.

Foster, J. B. 2009. *The Ecological Revolution: Making Peace with the Planet.* New York NY: Monthly Review.

Foster, J. B. and F. Magdoff. 2010. "What Every Environmentalist Needs to Know About Capitalism." *Monthly Review* 61, 10: 1–30.

Freeman, A. and A. Kliman. 2004. *The New Value Controversy and the Foundations of Economics.* Cheltenham UK: Edward Elgar.

Gerstein, I. 1976. "Production, Circulation and Value." *Economy and Society* 5, 3: 243–291.

Glyn, A. and B. Sutcliff. 1972. *Capitalism in Crisis.* New York NY: Pantheon.

Gordon, D., R. Edwards, and M. Reich. 1982. "Long Swings and Stages of Capitalism," in R. Gordon, R. Edwards, and M. Reich eds, *Segmented Work, Divided Workers: The Historical Transformation of Labor in the United States.* Cambridge UK: Cambridge University Press: 18–47.

Greenwood, D. and E. Wolff. 1992. "Changes in Wealth in the United States 1962–1983." *Journal of Population Economics* 5, 4: 261–288.

Hahnel, R. 2005. "Economic Justice." *Review of Radical Political Economics* 37, 2: 131–154.

Hahnel, R. 2006. "Exploitation: A Modern Approach." *Review of Radical Political Economics* 38, 2: 175–192.

Hahnel, R. 2007. "The Case Against Markets." *Journal of Economic Issues* 41, 4: 1139–1159.

Hahnel, R. 2013. "The Growth Imperative: Beyond Assuming Conclusions." *Review of Radical Political Economics* 45, 1: 24–41.

Hahnel, R. 2014a. *The ABCs of Political Economy: A Modern Approach*, 2nd edition. London UK: Pluto Press.

Hahnel, R. 2014b. "The Invisible Foot: A Tribute to E. K. Hunt." *Review of Radical Political Economics* 46, 1: 70–86.

Hahnel, R. 2016a. "A Tale of Three Theorems." *Review of Radical Political Economics*. Forthcoming.

Hahnel, R. 2016b. "Environmental Sustainability in a Sraffian Framework." *Review of Radical Political Economics*. Forthcoming.

Hahnel, R. 2017. *Income Distribution and Environmental Sustainability: A Sraffian Approach*. New York NY: Routledge.

Hahnel, R. and H. Sherman. 1982. "Income Distribution and the Business Cycle: Three Conflicting Hypotheses." *Journal of Economic Issues* 16, 1: 49–73.

Hahnel, R. and M. Albert. 1990. *Quiet Revolution in Welfare Economics*. Princeton NJ: Princeton University Press.

Harvey, D. 1996. *Justice, Nature, and the Geography of Difference*. Oxford UK: Blackwell Publishing.

Kalecki, M. 2009. *Theory of Economic Dynamics*, originally published in 1954. New York NY: Monthly Review.

Keynes, J. M. 1936. *The General Theory of Employment, Interest and Money*. London UK: MacMillan.

Kliman, A. 1996. "A Value-Theoretic Critique of the Okishio Theorem," in A. Freeman and G. Carchedi eds, *Marx and Non-Equilibrium Economics*. Cheltenham UK: Edward Elgar: 206–224.

Kliman, A. 1997. "The Okishio Theorem: An Obituary." *Review of Radical Political Economics* 29, 3: 42–50.

Kliman, A. 2001. "Simultaneous Valuation vs. the Exploitation Theory of Profit." *Capital and Class* 73: 97–112.

Kliman, A. 2007. *Reclaiming Marx's "Capital": A Refutation of the Myth of Inconsistency*. Lanham MD: Lexington Books.

Kliman, A. and T. McGlone. 1988. "The Transformation Non-problem and the Non-transformation Problem." *Capital and Class* 35: 56–83.

Kliman, A. and T. McGlone. "A Temporal Single-system Interpretation of Marx's Value Theory." *Review of Political Economy* 11, 1: 33–59.

Kliman, A. and N. Potts, eds. 2015. *Is Marx's Theory of Profits Right? The Simultaneous-Temporalist Debate*. Lanham MD: Lexington Books.

Kotlikoff, L. and L. Summers. 1981. "The Role of Intergenerational Transfers in Aggregate Capital Accumulation." *Journal of Political Economy* 89, 4: 706–732.

Kotz, D. 2015. *The Rise and Fall of Neoliberal Capitalism*. Cambridge MA: Harvard University Press.

Kotz, D., T. McDonough, and M. Reich. 1994. *Social Structures of Accumulation: The Political Economy of Growth and Crisis*. Cambridge UK: Cambridge University Press.

Kovel, J. 2002. *Enemy of Nature: The End of Capitalism or the End of the World*. London UK: ZED Books.

Kurz, H. and N. Salvadori. 1995. *Theory of Production: A Long-Period Analysis*. Cambridge UK: Cambridge University Press.

Laibman, D. 2000. "Rhetoric and Substance in Value Theory: An Appraisal of the New Orthodox Marxism." *Science and Society* 64: 310–332.

Luxemburg, R. 1951. *The Accumulation of Capital*, originally published in 1913. London UK: Routledge and Kegan Paul Ltd.

Marglin, S. 1981. *Growth, Distribution and Prices*. Cambridge MA: Harvard University Press.

Marx, K. 1967a. *Capital, Volume 1: A Critical Analysis of Capitalist Production*. New York NY: International Publishers, New World Paperbacks.

Marx, K. 1967b. *Capital, Volume 2: The Process of Circulation of Capital*. New York NY: International Publishers, New World Paperbacks.

Marx, K. 1967c. *Capital, Volume 3: The Process of Capitalist Production as a Whole*. New York NY: International Publishers, New World Paperbacks.

Marx, K. 1970. *The Economic and Philosophical Manuscripts of 1844*, revised edition. London UK: Lawrence and Wishart.

McDonough, T., M. Reich, and D. Kotz, eds. 2010. *Contemporary Capitalism and Its Crises*. Cambridge UK: Cambridge University Press.

McDonough, T., D. Kotz, and M. Reich, eds. 2014. *Social Structure of Accumulation Theory*, Volumes 1 and 2. Cheltenham UK: Edward Elgar.

Meek, R. 1973. *Studies in the Labor Theory of Value*. London UK: Lawrence and Wishart.

Minsky, H. 1986. *Stabilizing an Unstable Economy*. New York NY: McGraw-Hill.

Minsky, H. 1992. "The Financial Instability Hypothesis, Working Paper No. 74." Jerome Levy Economics Institute of Bard College.

Mohun, S. 1994. "A Re(in)statement of the Labour Theory of Value." *Cambridge Journal of Economics* 18: 391–412.

Mohun, S. 2003. "On the TSSI and the Exploitation Theory of Profit." *Capital and Class* 81: 85–102.

Mohun, S. 2004. "The Labour Theory of Value as Foundation for Empirical Investigations." *Metroeconomica* 55, 1: 65–95.

Mokyr, J. 1992. *Lever of Riches: Technological Creativity and Economic Progress*. Oxford UK: Oxford University Press.

Mongiovi, G. 2002. "Vulgar Economy in Marxian Garb: A Critique of Temporal Single System Marxism." *Review of Radical Political Economics* 34, 4: 393–416.

Moore, J. 2015. *Capitalism in the Web of Life: Ecology of the Accumulation of Capital*. London UK: Verso.

Morishima, M. 1974. "Marx in Light of Modern Economic Theory." *Econometrica* 42: 611–632.

Moseley, F. 1991. *The Falling Rate of Profit in the Postwar United States Economy*. London UK: Palgrave Macmillan.

Moseley, F. 2017. *Money and Totality: A Macro-Monetary Interpretation of Marx's Logic in Capital and the End of the 'Transformation Problem'*. Boston MA: Historical Materialism, Brill Press.

O'Connor, J. 1998. *Natural Causes: Essays in Ecological Marxism*. New York NY: Guilford.

Okishio, N. 1961. "Technical Changes and the Rate of Profit." *Kobe University Economic Review* 7: 85–99.

Persky, J. and J. Alberro. 1978. "Technical Innovation and the Dynamics of the Profit Rate." University of Illinois, Chicago Circle, Department of Economics.

Piketty, T. 2014. *Capital in the Twenty First Century.* Cambridge MA: Harvard University Press.

Roemer, J. 1981. *Analytical Foundations of Marxian Economic Theory.* Cambridge UK: Cambridge University Press.

Romer, P. 1990. "Endogenous Technological Change." *Journal of Political Economy* 98, 5: 83–84.

Samuelson, P. 1971. "Understanding the Marxian Notion of Exploitation: A Summary of the So-Called Transformation Problem between Marxian Values and Competitive Prices." *Journal of Economic Literature* 9, 2: 399–431.

Shaikh, A. 1977. "Marx's Theory of Value and the Transformation Problem," in J. Schwartz, ed., *The Subtle Anatomy of Capitalism.* New York NY: Goodyear Publishing: 106–139.

Shaikh, A. 1978a. "An Introduction to the History of Crisis Theories," in *U.S. Capitalism in Crisis.* Union of Radical Political Economics URPE.

Shaikh, A. 1978b. "Political Economy and Capitalism: Notes on Dobb's Theory of Crisis." *Cambridge Journal of Economics* 2: 233–251.

Shaikh, A. 2016. *Capitalism: Competition, Conflict, Crisis.* Oxford UK: Oxford University Press.

Skillman, G. 2001. "Anomalies in the 'Temporal Single-system' Interpretation of Marx's Value Theory," mimeo, Wesleyan University.

Smith, A. 1776. *An Inquiry into the Nature and Causes of the Wealth of Nations.*

Sraffa, P. 1960. *Production of Commodities by Means of Commodities.* Cambridge UK: Cambridge University Press.

Sweezy, P. 1942. *Theory of Capitalist Development: Principles of Marxian Political Economy.* New York NY: Monthly Review.

Thurow, L. 1996. *The Future of Capitalism: How Today's Economic Forces Will Shape the Future.* New York NY: William Morrow.

Veneziani, R. 2004. "The Temporal Single-System Interpretation of Marx's Economics: A Critical Evaluation." *Metroeconomica* 55, 1: 96–114.

Weisskopf, T. 1979. "Marxian Crisis Theory and the Rate of Profit in the Postwar U.S. Economy." *Cambridge Journal of Economics* 3, 4: 341–378.

Weisskopf, T. 1992. "Marxian Crisis Theory and the Contradictions of Late Twentieth-Century Capitalism." *Rethinking Marxism* 4, 4: 70–93.

INDEX

Note: Figures are indicated by page numbers in *italics*.